The Unseen Politics of
Public Housing

The Unseen Politics of Public Housing

Resident Councils, Communities, and Change

Tiffany Chenault

LEXINGTON BOOKS
Lanham • Boulder • New York • London

Published by Lexington Books
An imprint of The Rowman & Littlefield Publishing Group, Inc.
4501 Forbes Boulevard, Suite 200, Lanham, Maryland 20706
www.rowman.com

Unit A, Whitacre Mews, 26-34 Stannary Street, London SE11 4AB

British Library Cataloguing in Publication Information Available

Library of Congress Cataloging-in-Publication Data

Chenault, Tiffany, 1974-
The unseen politics of public housing : resident councils, communities, and change / Tiffany Chenault.
pages cm.
Includes bibliographical references and index.
ISBN 978-0-7391-6506-5 (cloth : alk. paper) – ISBN 978-0-7391-6508-9 (ebook)
1. Public housing–United States. 2. Low-income housing–United States. 3. United States–Race relations. 4. Sociology, Urban–United States. I. Title.
HD7288.78.U5C44 2015
363.5'850973–dc23
2015010212

Printed in the United States of America

Contents

Start of the Journey

In truth I don't remember thinking much about public housing because it was so beyond my world. I didn't know anyone who had lived in public housing, nor had I ever visited a public housing community. How I made the transition from indifference to or stereotypical perspectives on public housing to research on the topic actually began with a very simple act: helping a friend.

After my friend Derek said his wife needed volunteers at the Resolution Action Center (RAC), I began my training, training that would become the first step in my journey toward a deeper understanding of public housing communities. For over ten years the center has trained hundreds of people in the principles of conflict resolution and has provided mediation for over seven hundred disputes.[1]

To increase the community's capacity to resolve disputes effectively, the RAC conducts several programs and workshops throughout the state. One community with which the center has worked especially closely is public housing. To support such work, the center has received a Resident Opportunities and Self Sufficiency (ROSS) grant from the Department of Housing and Urban Development (HUD), a type of funding developed from the Public Housing Reform Act (PHRA) of 1998, which initiated reforms aimed at creating mixed-income communities. The program initiatives are intended to promote self-sufficiency, enhance quality of life for public housing residents, and create personal responsibility in communities. With this grant money, the RAC was supposed to increase the ability of public housing residents to resolve conflicts effectively and nonviolently, thereby enhancing their ability to become economically self-sufficient and improving their quality of life.

My job was to enhance the general mediation model so as to make it appropriate for the types of disputes typically found in public housing neighborhoods. As I started working on my section of the grant, two problems arose: I discovered that the conflicts found in public housing differed from the disputes I had mediated and that the mediation strategies I had learned were not an appropriate cultural "fit."[2] In order to create a mediation model, I realized that I needed a better understanding of the context in which the conflicts arose. After all, as a sociologist I have learned that attitudes, behaviors, values, and beliefs are "always situated within and shaped by the social context of relationships among people who share the experience of belonging to a community" (N. Smith, Littlejohns, and Thompson 2001, 34). No doubt this is true of conflicts as well.

As a result of this realization, my ideas about a new mediation model metamorphosed into an understanding of community within a public housing context. This topic, I reasoned, should be a feasible project, since the RAC worked closely with the Ridgeway Housing Authority,[3] a situation that gave me access to and a legitimate standing with public housing residents and administrators.

My background reading for this research reassured me that my focus on community within the public housing context was indeed on track. For example, when I read literature about public housing distributed by the Department of Housing and Urban Development (HUD), I noticed that the agency itself stresses the concept of "community." In its mission statement, strategic goals and planning document, as well as throughout its website, HUD uses such terms as "community development," "community empowerment," and "self-sufficiency through community." Even in its fiscal budget report, HUD writes that it offers "new opportunities for communities nationwide to generate renewal growth and prosperity through programs that promote local decision-making" (2004 HUD Budget Executive Summary).

As I looked again at the HUD writings that emphasized the concept of community, I had to ask myself: What do they mean by "community" and how do they expect "community" to be developed? I began to wonder whether HUD's consistent, repeated use of the term actually means there really is *no* community in public housing at present or that the concept is an idealized one, potential yet currently unachieved. Or is the type of community that currently exists in public housing a negative one that needs constant fixing or "tweaking" because it does not in its present form meet HUD's or society's norms and standards of community? These and other questions led me to realize that I could not study "the community" without a better idea of what is meant by community within the public housing context.

I began this project with the goal of including all the public housing communities in the city of Ridgeway.[4] Through my affiliation with the RAC, I met with several of the managers at the different public housing sites, attended site-based, joint resident council and other general community meetings, spoke with the executive director and members of the housing authority, and began going to resident council meetings. After a time, my face became known in all the public housing communities, and I realized I had cultivated a sizable and valuable network of contacts.

In qualitative research, selection of a case can be based on a variety of criteria. For example, a case can be selected because it portrays something uncommon or is considered typical, because it is rich in information or is political, because it offers accessible and readily available informants, or because of the intensity of the phenomenon being studied (Merriam 2001; Patton 1990; Stake 2000). To select my community, Rivertown,[5] I used practical and personal reasons, both reasons having positive implications for the quality of the data collected. My choice was practical: this location offered me easy access to a nearby community where my presence was already established through my work with the RAC. I knew that having such access would allow me to understand and study the uniqueness and complexities of this particular community in public housing in great detail with far greater intensity than researching a community without such access.

My choice was also personal. Qualitative researchers are well aware of the importance of status characteristics and how they affect every aspect of qualitative research (Bailey 1996). My status characteristics certainly were a factor in how I selected Rivertown as my subject of study. Of the managers I met, only two were African American women. The manager of Rivertown, Vanessa,[6] was the younger of the two women, and as a twenty-eight-year-old black woman, I found that I was more comfortable with her. Our rapport seemed to provide the basis for a more fruitful research experience.

With my research interest refined from a general study of community in public housing to the more limited issues of how community is defined and developed in Rivertown, I started conducting preliminary interviews. Although I had decided on Rivertown, I thought insight from the other managers of the different housing communities might provide my study with essential background. One of my first interviews was with Tyler Jones.[7] While Tyler provided useful information regarding several areas of investigation, he repeatedly returned our conversation to the topic of "site-based meetings," saying such things as the following:

> "At site-based meetings . . . you know and see what our community wants."
> "Site based means everything is done."
> "Site-based meetings have full control over our properties."
> "You need to come to a site-based meeting."

When I reread my field notes prior to analysis, it was clear that I had become increasingly frustrated by Tyler's single-minded fixation on site-based meetings. I had written:

> "That man gave me a headache, I didn't get the response I wanted and he kept talking about site-based meetings."

> "Almost every other word was site-based meetings. I asked about a shooting death that happened in the community and he talked about the resident council."

> "I can't believe this man asked me to help out with his site-based meetings. He wants to put me to work."

> "This man scheduled the next site-based meeting around me because he wants me there. I don't think so."

Today, I am somewhat embarrassed to read my own reactions to his emphasis on site-based meetings. Fortunately, however, I know such feelings are not uncommon among qualitative researchers. For example, Van Maanen (in Van Maanen, Dabbs, and Faulkner 1982, 107) admitted how embarrassed he was that his early field notes, conducted at the beginning of his study, expressed his "loathing" for police.

Although each of the communities I initially considered were vastly different, as I interviewed other managers, I in fact began to discover a relatively widespread emphasis on site-based meetings. At the advice of these managers I decided to attend some site-based meetings to gather background material.

Attendees at the site-based meetings generally consisted of resident council members, the manager, maintenance personnel, and community-oriented police enforcement (COPE) officers. After attending several site-based meetings at the various communities, however, I noticed that forming the heart of these meetings were members of the resident councils. The nonresidents who attended the site-based meeting directed the majority of their comments and questions toward council members. In fact, it was not uncommon for the resident council members to be the only members of the community in attendance. It seemed clear to me that if site-based meetings were the source of insight into this community, the lens would be the resident council.

As I continued my reading of HUD materials, I noticed that they too stressed the importance of resident councils as a means to develop community; resident councils were, as it turns out, initially organized and supported by the agency in order to involve residents more fully in building their communities. HUD and the housing authority (HA) also have actual policies that not only stress but support resident councils.

After attending the site-based meetings and reviewing more HUD policies, I could not shake the feeling that HUD was expecting a great deal from the resident councils. I begin to wonder if the resident council in Rivertown was able to build community as HUD implied they should, and if they were, what activities did they engage in that led to community building? If they were not, why not? Was their role purely symbolic? I was curious if they had a role in creating the policies and laws that stress community building and rules that governed them. I found myself wanting to know if the various parties—HUD and housing authority officials, and, the council members themselves—agreed that seeking community was an important goal for the resident council and if following the policies was the best way for the resident council to meet the goals. Was there agreement among all parties in their interpretation of the policies and the practices of the resident council, or were there areas of disagreement? With these and other questions, I had finally arrived at the beginning of this sociological research.

This book is my attempt to describe and explain HUD's expectations for the resident council as an active agent for community building and the actual practices of the resident council. I argue that policies and regulations of resident councils, which exist to support the effectiveness of the resident council in creating and implementing community building, self-sufficiency, and empowerment activities and goals in a public housing community, may do more harm than good. Further, I suggest that using critical race theory can explain the interpretation, implementation, and enforcement of resident council laws and policies.

PUBLIC HOUSING: A DIFFERENT BALL GAME

Public housing has received a great deal of attention by researchers. The focus of this book is on public housing "projects," not on low-income or poor neighborhoods, Section 8 housing, or neighborhoods in general. Such omissions are vital to an accurate depiction of the setting being studied: low-income neighborhoods are not always public housing neighborhoods; Section 8 and public housing are both funded by the Department of Housing and Urban Development (HUD), but they are two different types of housing programs; and "neighborhoods in general" refers to a motley collection of types.

Compared to the other forms of housing mentioned above, public housing is an altogether different "ball game." It is unique because the different and complex legal and administrative structures that govern it lead to different dynamics and rules that do not exist in poor and other general neighborhoods.

The literature that seems the most relevant involves that which has focused on tenant/resident management in public housing. Tenant/resident management in public housing involves tenants of public housing communities coming together to improve the conditions of their communities. In that same fashion, resident councils are public housing tenants participating in improving their community. Thus, the brief history of tenant management that follows can provide a background for this research on resident councils.

IMPORTANCE OF TENANT MANAGEMENT

The ideal of tenant participation in public housing developed from the social upheaval from the civil rights and welfare rights movements of the 1960s. Tenant management in public housing first appeared thirty-three years ago in Boston and St. Louis, where residents—in jeopardy of losing their homes because of mismanagement from the housing authority—took control of the situation (HUD 1992). In 1971, in Boston's Bromley Heath Project, residents became managers and assumed the duties of acquiring health and social services for residents. In St. Louis, tenant management developed as a result of the 1969 public housing rent strike (Peterman 1996). Between 1973 and 1975, five separate developments in St. Louis became resident managed.

In 1975, the HUD, along with the Ford Foundation, collaborated on a National Tenant Management Demonstration Program (NTMDP). The purposes of NTMDP were twofold: to establish new resident management corporations and to evaluate their effectiveness for improving public housing management (HUD 1992).

Evaluating the effectiveness of tenant management, the Manpower Demonstration Research Corporation concluded that resident management corporations cost too much money, could not be applied universally to other housing "projects," and recommended ending the demonstration program (Peterman 1996). Ten years later, HUD evaluated the effectiveness of resident management in public housing. Its evaluation found that under a full-service resident management corporation (RMC), residents had a "more positive perception of the quality of life at their development" (HUD 1992, 5).

Cochran Gardens is an example of a positive impact of resident managers. Located in St. Louis, Cochran Gardens is a twelve-building complex with 1,900 residents. The buildings were plagued by the smells of urine, bullet holes, and drugs were being sold and used openly. Because of the actions of resident managers who took responsibility and control of the buildings, Cochran Gardens was transformed into a community with clean floors and painted walls, where minor repairs made the buildings more livable (Wilkerson 1988). At Kenilworth-Parkside in Washington, D.C., resident managers took over operations "of social services in the community, formed a crime patrol, developed a drug center, and established tenant-run businesses in the development such as a co-op store, a thrift shop, and a beauty salon" (Carlile 1990, 65).

To encourage RMCs in public housing developments, in 1987 Congress amended the Housing Act of 1937, with Section 122 of the Housing and

Community Development Act (HUD 1992). Subpart B of Part 964, entitled Tenant Participation, describes in detail the requirements for the formation of a resident management corporation. Additionally, Congress set forth the regulations governing the relationship between a housing authority and a resident management corporation in the *Code of Federal Regulations* (24 C.F.R. 964.120: Resident Management Corporation Requirements). Resident management corporations can operate in conjunction with resident councils or in the absence of resident councils.

Resident councils are entitled to the same laws, responsibilities, and privileges of the RMC with two key exceptions. First, they do not have managerial control of their public housing community, which means they cannot hire or fire people or be considered employees of the housing authority. Second, under the laws of each state, resident management corporations are incorporated, nonprofit organizations, whereas resident councils receive funding only from the housing authority and HUD, such as stipends for members who agree to volunteer their time and services. In addition to those differences, both bodies are supposed to help build communities and empower residents in public housing. Some public housing communities have both an RMC and a resident council, some have an RMC and not a resident council, and others just have a resident council. The size, resources, situation, and the relationship between the residents and housing authority dictate whether there is a resident council, RMC, or both.

Rivertown, the public housing community in this study, has a resident council instead of a resident management corporation. All the public housing communities in the city of Ridgeway (where this study takes place) only have resident councils.

RESIDENT COUNCILS: WHY DO THIS RESEARCH?

Although there is a significant amount of literature on public housing, resident management corporations, and tenant associations, little research has focused exclusively on resident councils. My research will fill this gap. It will differ in four essential ways from previous research.

First, few studies have examined the impact of resident councils as an effective tool for building community in public housing. Studies have examined the impact of tenant management (Carlile 1990; Peterman 1996; Lane 1995), home ownership (Vale 1998), community development and organization (Vale 1998; Ferguson and Dickens 1999: Chaskin 2001), and asset building (G. Green and Haines 2002), but these examinations differ markedly from a study of the polices, rules, histories, and structures of resident councils.

Second, historical context and spatial context matter. Structural conditions, such as economic, political, and cultural factors, powerfully affect the internal dynamics of minority and poor community development, and these are often historically and spatially contingent (Wilson 1987, 1996; Massey and Denton 1993). Much of the research on public housing has long been done in metropolitan areas, such as the "Chicago projects" (Gotham 2000b; Hensen and James 1987). Studies conducted in Chicago and other metropolitan cities may not, however, be relevant to those undertaken in "the state"[8] because community and cultural dynamics, as well as political, economic, and legislative policies, will be vastly different.

The majority of the 1.2 million people who live in public housing do not live in large urban areas with thousands of people confined to a certain space. The majority of public housing units (90 percent) have fewer than five hundred units (Schwartz 2015). These smaller units and the people that live in them tend to go unnoticed.

RIVERTOWN: ETHNOGRAPHIC CASE STUDY

This ethnographic case study focuses on explaining and understanding the factors and constraints that exist between HUD's expectations for the resident council as an active agent for community building and the actual practices of the resident council. To explain the disjunction—in fact, to determine if such disjunctions identified by Rivertown council members are real. Using the tenets of critical race theory allows us to understand what forces—either real or imagined, structural or cultural—prevent the resident council from being an effective agent for change in the public housing community. Since over one million live in public housing with billions of dollars being invested, it is important to understand why some " programs" are not working. Through the voices of the fourteen "cast of voices" from the residents, resident council members, managers, housing authority officials, and community workers we get a snapshot as to why policies, especially public housing policies, are not always effective and what can be done to make them so.

An ethnographic case study provides "an intensive, holistic description and analysis of a single instance, phenomenon, a social unit," the aim of which is to understand and uncover "interaction of significant factors characteristic of the phenomenon" (Merriam 2001, 27). A case study is defined as a "specific, unique, bounded system" (Patton 2002, 447). For instance, a case could be a teacher, a program, a specific policy, or an organization, among other things. An ethnographic case study allows me to better understand aspects of particular organizational policies that apply to the resident council; its purpose is not to develop or test new theory (Berg 2001). Data for case studies include interviews, observations, content analysis, and contextual information (Patton 2002; Merriam 2001; Berg 2001).

I spent over two years with the Rivertown Resident Council. I rely on in-depth interviews, participation observations, and field notes with fourteen individuals either associated with the resident council or residents themselves. Four active council members, three community agency workers, three managers, two housing authority officials, and two residents to make the case for understanding the dynamics of resident participation and community engagement. The fourteen individuals herein described all play major roles in this ethnographic case study. Each has an essential hand in the effective functioning of the Rivertown Resident Council. Their backgrounds, perceptions, experiences, and interactions with each other, as well as with residents, shape the council's development and determine how it will implement community-building activities.

OVERVIEW OF PUBLIC HOUSING AND RESIDENT COUNCILS

Sociology has long been interested in the reciprocal relationship between social structures (macro-level phenomena: institutions, economy, educational system) and social processes (micro-level phenomena: individuals, cultural experiences, behaviors, and attitudes). A way to understand the bidirectional link between micro- and macro-level phenomena is through laws and policies, both of which impact how people experience their lives. At the same time, they can be shaped by individual life experiences. For example, the overt racism that African Americans experienced in employment, education, and housing shaped civil rights laws and policies of the 1950s and 1960s, which legally prohibited discrimination in these areas.

One way to analyze this is through the lens (and voices) of a resident council in public housing. Public housing is an altogether different "ball game." It is unique because the different and complex legal and administrative structures that govern it lead to different dynamics and rules that do not exist in poor and other general neighborhoods. Members of the resident council are expected to improve the quality of life and the living environment for all community residents. They must do so, however, against the backdrop of a negative racialized history of residential segregation, discrimination, and mismanagement of government funding. In an effort to prevent a return to the checkered past of public housing, the *Code of Federal Regulations* (CFR) stresses a strong partnership among resident councils, HAs, and HUD. Tenant concerns are primary, and the purpose of the resident council is to act as the conduit between such concerns and the administration.

Legally and theoretically, the *Code of Federal Regulations* gives resident council members—when working in conjunction with the housing authority—some autonomy, support, and resources to improve their communities however they see fit.

These rules and regulations (1) define the role of the resident council to the community, (2) define the role of the housing authority officials to the council, (3) determine the structure of the council meetings, and (4) indicate the amount and type of funding they receive. The policies and regulations of resident councils exist to support the effectiveness of the resident council in creating and implementing community building, self-sufficiency, and empowerment activities and goals in the community.

Despite the federal rules and regulations and the Green Book, the resident council was not meeting the expectations of housing officials. Nor were the housing officials doing what the council expected of them. Disconnections existed between the resident council, managers, housing authority officials, and community workers, which may have led to system failure. The disjunctions were not discrete, but rather overlapping and interwoven into each other.

I identified seven areas of disjunction between and within the housing authority, community workers, managers, and resident council members of Rivertown. The seven major areas of disjunction in Rivertown I identified were (1) focus on children, (2) leadership, (3) snitching, (4) responsibilities, (5) manager/managerial styles, (6) meeting dynamics, and (7) HUD structure and priorities.

In addition, the policies created to "assist" the council in helping its community have done more harm than good. Some members of the council, as well as managers and community workers, thought the policies were discriminatory, and treated the residents unequally. Others members believed the housing authority really had all the control and that council members did not have any control over the communities they were chosen to serve. Policies designed to promote and encourage self-sufficiency actually meant more work for the managers, housing authority officials, and community workers, which in turn meant such groups would be unable to help the council. As a result, the policies themselves have created a vicious cycle. While HUD wants to promote self-sufficiency and encourages residents to join the council, many of the very policies it has enacted to achieve these goals have caused that council to be less effective.

STRUCTURE OF BOOK

Chapter 1 of this book begins with the location of Rivertown, ethnographic stories of the council members, and dynamics of the community and summarizes why the members joined the council.

Chapter 2 offers a history and understanding of the *Code of Federal Regulations* (CFR). I discuss the roles and responsibilities of the housing authority officials (managers, community workers, housing authority management) to ensure the success of the council and their mission and follow the CFR.

Chapters 3, 4, 5, and 6 are examples of disjuncture between the council members and the housing authority officials. These chapters detail unclear responsibility and how policies and lack of implementation got in the way of the council's success. This was demonstrated by the focus on children, funding, communication, location, policies, and managerial styles.

Chapter 7 offers policy recommendations for building resident participation in public housing.

NOTES

1. Quite simply, mediation is an informal and voluntary process for working through interpersonal or group conflicts; through it, people can resolve conflict without going to court or hiring a lawyer.

2. The mediation strategies I learned were appropriate for dealing with the business and corporate culture, tenants and landlords in the private sector, custody issues, and divorces.

3. The city of Ridgeway is where this study takes place. The Ridgeway Housing Authority owns and operates all the public housing facilities in the city. Ridgeway is a pseudonym.

4. There are between eight and twelve public housing communities in the city of Ridgeway. I am not giving the exact number as a small effort to disguise the location of Ridgeway. Issues of confidentiality are discussed in more detail in chapter 2.

5. Rivertown is a pseudonym. A discussion of this and all pseudonyms and confidentiality issues is presented in chapter 2.

6. Vanessa is a pseudonym.

7. Tyler Jones is a pseudonym.

8. "The state" is the pseudonym for that state and city in which this research is being done.

Chapter One

Welcome to Rivertown

Constructed in 1972, Rivertown is the fourth-largest public housing community in the city of Ridgeway, with 150 apartment units. It is nestled in a valley of rolling hills and trees, a location antithetical to the traditional conception of "public housing."

As I first approached Rivertown, two things became clear immediately: this community was located in a residential neighborhood, and it was the farthest away from other public housing communities in the city. In my mind, public housing was urban, concrete, brick, noisy, and involved high-rise structures, a conception that is perhaps shared by others. The location of this community was definitely suburban. Rivertown did not look like any of the complexes I had seen either in person or represented through the media, real or fictionalized.

What attracted me to the community was not only the manager but also the diversity among the residents. There were 439 total residents living in Rivertown: 183 whites (42 percent of the total population), 192 black (44 percent), 8 Native American (2 percent), and 56 Asian (12 percent). The racial composition of Rivertown has a higher African American and Asian population than either the city of Ridgeway or the state in which it resides. The majority of the residents' income in Rivertown is derived from SSI (Supplemental Security Income), Social Security, TANF (Temporary Assistance for Needy Families), and child support; some had no income at all. Heads of households ranged in age from nineteen to sixty-four.

Driving down the two lanes of Walker Street en route to Rivertown, I passed a Subway restaurant, gas station, Laundromat, convenience store, and several colorful houses on the left side of the road. On the right side of Walker Street, a river runs parallel to the road, and there I observed people fishing and gathering for recreation. If one passes the left-facing entrance to

Rivertown and continues down Walker Street, one would find a major grocery store, a Dollar Store, and a fire station. The end of Walker Street is marked by a fork in the road: the right turn takes drivers by an industrial park within the city limits; the left turn, however, leaves the city limits and enters Ridge County.

From Walker Street, one enters Rivertown by turning left onto Mill Street, the complex's main entrance. As I drove around the community I noticed that, besides the Mill Street entrance, Rivertown is composed of two main streets: Lemontree Drive and Baywater Drive. The community is laid out in an L shape, with Baywater at the bottom of the hill and Lemontree at the top. Along Mill Street, single housing units can be found on the left, and the community building is on the right.

In this important community building, one finds the community room, as well as offices for the property manager, maintenance, and resident council. In front of the community building is an open field and a playground set. The latter item provided a point of departure for the rest of the journey. Fully equipped with swings, slides, and other paraphernalia to provide the children of Rivertown with hours of fun, this playground set is also brightly colored in yellows, reds, and oranges. Its happy hues provided a startling contrast to the bleak apartment buildings of Rivertown.

The physical design and color of the buildings spoke loudly for the fact that, despite the picturesque surroundings, this was indeed public housing. I came upon several buildings with brick foundations, either painted a mustard yellow or covered with dark brown stucco. As I drove closer, I saw stains on the buildings that suggested leaks. Had something inside leaked and run down the exteriors? Whatever the origin, this mark, which ran down several of the buildings, made them look dirty, dark, and nasty. The buildings themselves did not physically or aesthetically match the quality of the single-unit houses on Mill Street. They were built closely together. Some possessed shuttered windows, while others did not—or either the shutters were barely hanging on. Some doors revealed peeling paint; others, graffiti. The physicality of Rivertown alone made it stick out like a sore thumb. Once inside the complex, one saw quickly that it looked very much like "typical" public housing.

As I continued to drive around on Baywater and Lemontree, I noticed the quality (or lack thereof) of the landscaping: some yards were covered sparsely with grass, while others appeared to be mere dirt, with no grass or flowers to alleviate the brownness. Moreover, the residents seemed to have done little to add the sorts of personal touches that make a house a home. There were no door signs proclaiming "The Joneses" or "The Smiths," nor did I see any house or yard fixtures. In fact, besides a couple of wind chimes hanging from someone's porch, and a minimum of exterior decorations scattered on top and the bottom of the hill, I saw nothing that made one apartment distinguishable from another. The two big Dumpsters that service the complex were overflowing with trash and dirt. Needless to say, my first impressions of this place as antithetical to traditional conceptions of public housing changed dramatically. Within this physical location reside most of the individuals central to this research. This is a place many called home.

Physical design and aesthetics aside, Rivertown is a place where people must live. Its residents did not grow up aspiring to live in public housing, but they arrived at this destination nonetheless. Their pasts, as well as their present situations and hopes for the future, inform who they are.

RIVERTOWN RESIDENT COUNCIL

One of the first council members I met, Sam, had been living in Rivertown for almost twenty years—which is why I call him the senior statesman on the council and in the community. When I first met him, I thought he was merely a flirty old man. He would ask for hugs, offer me something to drink, sit close to me at council meetings. At first I was annoyed, but as I got to know him, I realized that he was just a friendly, sweet, kind, and loving man who craved interaction with people. Sam was also generous—and a gentleman. He would go out of his way and spend his own money to buy me salads or a diet soda. He would also do that for the other women on the council.

Sam was African American, about 5'6", with short salt-and-pepper hair. Although he was just fifty-seven, he looked much older—you could see a hard life reflected in his face and in his big brown eyes, which were sometimes glassy and tinged with red.

Before they changed the resident council meetings to Friday, Sam's day off, he would come directly from work, despite having just finished a long day as a truck driver with Ridgeway's sanitation crew. He had been working for the city for over twenty years, and four of those years he spent as a truck driver. As Sam stated, "The majority of my years working for the city were spent behind the truck. . . . I worked behind the truck, picking up trash." Sam had a strong work ethic. He would be the first to tell you that he had worked all his life, and he took pride in what he did. He told me that "even when I was drinking, I still worked." He was even given an award for his service and dedication to the job. The city had a dinner for all the civil employees, and as a thank-you for his years of service, he received a watch.

Sam is the classic example of someone that I would call "just on the edge, just on the cusp" between middle and lower class. Before he moved to Rivertown, he and his family lived in a rented house. The landlord did not want to take care of maintenance issues that occurred in the house, and as a means of ridding himself of his tenants, he increased the rent to a price that Sam's family could not afford. Sam recalled:

[The] landlord didn't want to fix nothing and, uh,[1] we had to move out because, the rent went up, and he couldn't tell us why. We lived on 5292 Cherry
Lane. You could cut the heat on in the morning and you go to work and come
back and there would still be no heat. And the water, you'll have so much
water in the tub, and when they found out what was wrong with the problem,
humm, they told the landlord they have to fix it and he fixed it but, huh, he
went up on our rent and didn't tell us. And we were going to go to court. He
didn't want to go into battle. He sent us a moving notice instead.
     Then we moved over to southwest for about three to four years until that
guy, hmmm, he got the landlord over there, and another company took over.
They went up on our rent. And I said too much rent, so we landed down here
[Rivertown] and we've been here ever since.

Sam and his wife raised six children in Rivertown. At one point he
planned to move his family from Rivertown and purchase a home of their
own. They had even gone through one of the housing authority's funding
programs to finance a $70,000 loan, but before he could sign the contract, he
was injured on the job—his left hip popped out of its socket. Sam refused to
have the surgery that would correct this problem because he didn't want to
miss work. As he put it, "I've worked all my life, I've never taken a day off."
Despite his reluctance, though, eventually Sam had to undergo the surgery,
which indeed kept him unemployed for two years. Since he didn't know the
extent of his injury and he didn't want to go in debt, his plans for moving his
family out of Rivertown changed: "We had to put looking for a house on
hold." Sam's injury and surgery occurred in 1998, the same year he was
asked to volunteer with the resident council. Over time, he went from volunteering to being a member of the council.

Sam was one of the six members of the duly elected resident council in
Rivertown.

Linda, the unofficial president of the council, was the other member who
was a permanent, stable fixture of the council. Other members may come and
go, but Sam and Linda were the "mainstays." Linda is a white woman in her
late fifties. A thin but curvy woman, she had a head full of short gray hair, a
face full of winkles, and a strong, straightforward attitude. She drank coffee
and smoked incessantly. An active grandmother, she took her grandchildren
to school and to their extracurricular activities, making sure their needs were
met. Until five and a half years ago, Linda lived with her oldest daughter and
granddaughter and still worked at the packing plant. Because of her depression and panic attacks, Linda could not live by herself. When her daughter
died of cancer, she tried living with her older child. As she described it,

I can't live with them, they're young [*laughs*]; after Pat passed away I moved
in with Belinda.[2] And, we get along great and we're real close and I get along
with the children. Someone came knocking on her door at 1:30 in the morning.
They come in and they start "talking." I hear all this going on. "I told her I had

to get out of here." Her boyfriend wouldn't come over at night because he didn't want to disrespect me, to come in after dark. This was creating a problem for me because she had to go out the house to meet him. She said it wasn't bothering her but it was bothering me. It was little things. Like with my things, you know, like if I lay a piece of paper down here, four days later, I want that piece of piece of paper laying where I left it.

Having nowhere else to go, not being able to work, and being a burden on her children, Linda was forced to live in public housing. She elaborated:

Because my daughter passed away and I didn't have nowhere else to live and hmmm, my caseworker that worked with her suggest that I continue to work, but then after she passed away I wasn't able to go to work. I didn't want to move here [Rivertown] but I had learned to deal with life and be independent.

Linda's daughter's death put her in a severe depression. At the same time, she became the legal guardian of her granddaughter. In addition, her younger daughter, Belinda, gave her custody of her son, since she was not in a position to take care of him herself.

Linda had been living in Rivertown for five and a half years, and she had been on the council for three of those years. Everybody in the community called Linda "Granny." She helped out and took care of other people's kids. Despite the fact that Linda's main income derived from Supplemental Security Income (SSI), she routinely invited children over for dinner or sleepovers.

When Linda went to her first resident council meeting, she found out that children were to be the primary focus of members' activities. Describing her first meeting, she said, "And so I attended one of the meetings that they were having and they were talking about all these things that could be done here with the children and you could get a group of these kids together and take 'em to a movie or we could do all kinds of things." Because Linda already helped the children in the community, the objective of the council met with her approval. (Actually, the reason why most of the residents join the council was to focus on the children in the community.)

Jessica, another member of the council, was a twenty-eight-year-old white woman who had lived in Rivertown for two years. Shoulder-length black hair and pretty blue eyes highlighted her youthful face. In fact, when I first met her, she appeared so young that I had a difficult time believing she was a mother of four, three of whom lived with her at the complex (the fourth lived with his father). Before she moved to Rivertown, she lived for a year and a half at a family shelter. Both of Jessica's ex-husbands cheated on her and, worse, were abusive. For her, moving to Rivertown was another step toward getting back on her feet. She adamantly stated:

I have a plan and a lot of stuff to work on, like my license and getting a car and cleaning up my credit and stuff like that.

Jessica hoped to move out of Rivertown in a couple of years. She wanted to work as a physical therapist, which meant further schooling. Jessica indicated that her conception of the council was bound to what it could do for children and the community as a whole: "Basically they're here for this community, to help them and do stuff for the kids." She was on the council for six months.

Like Jessica, Sam interpreted the purpose of the council to meet the needs of the children: "Our job is to make sure that like you know the community is involved before we make the decisions we make and you know we have dances we have something for the kids—plays and stuff like that there, any kind of games and stuff like that there." Pebe, another member of the council, joined because she "wanted to do something for the children—they need activities and things to do here because the parents aren't doing anything."

Pebe was a twenty-seven-year-old African American woman, married with three children. At first I thought she had four children, the way she talked about her bluebirds:

> If I'm feeling sad or depressed, it's like my bird, my bluebird Christie, and she will walk over to the end of my stick or wherever I'm at and she'll just whistle for me to come over . . . she'll just sit there and whistle and do her head side to side, that's my baby [*big smile*].

Unlike Jessica, Pebe seemed much older than her age. She was very mature, insightful, and calm. She lived in Rivertown for a year and a half before she left and found a house she could rent. Just like Jessica, Pebe viewed Rivertown as a temporary fix because living in Rivertown provided her family with a means to get back on their feet:

> We came here [Rivertown] just to better ourselves and to get all our other bills caught up so once we get out of here we'll be financial stable.

Although both Pebe and her husband worked, financial problems and illness brought her family to Rivertown. Before they moved to public housing, they were renting a house; but her husband, who suffered from epilepsy, experienced a seizure, which forced him to leave work. Because of the type of job he had, he could not receive disability for his seizures. This only added to the family's financial stress.

In addition, one of Pebe's children had been diagnosed as manic-depressive. As a result, she had to quit her job so she could stay at home with her son and give him the special care and attention he needed. Pebe was on the council for six months until she moved out of Rivertown. Despite the various circumstances and situations that brought people to Rivertown, there was a need for tenant participation in their community. Linda, Sam, Pebe, and Jessica volunteered their time and energy to make the community "better for the children." This council had a mixture of residents with a diversity of age, race, and abilities that they brought to the council.

Resident councils are created to include residents' voices and life experiences in the local decision-making and community development processes in public housing communities. The hope is that including residents and resident council members in the creation and dissemination of public housing laws and policies will promote self-sufficiency and community empowerment. In other words, resident council policies are supposed to include and reflect the life experiences of the residents of public housing. Despite their busy lives, the members of Rivertown wanted to do activities and programs that could benefit the children in their community. It is important to understand that community dynamics plays a role in participation in public housing.

DIVISION IN RIVERTOWN

At first, the people who lived in Rivertown were, in my mind, universally the same: poor or low income. They lived in public housing due to experiencing economic hardships. But what I soon realized was that the stereotypes that nonpoor people have about residents of public housing were also internalized by the residents and council members of Rivertown. Research conducted by Gotham and Brumley demonstrated that "urban spaces shape and condition how individuals and groups think and conceive of themselves, cultivate and develop personal and collective identities and contest as well as reinforce prevailing meanings of race, class, gender, sexual orientation and other social inequalities" (2002, 269). The council members tended to distance themselves from the stigmatized "project identity." Regardless of the fact that they, too, lived in public housing, they did not conceive of themselves as being like "those other people" who do not care or "those people" who do not take care of their children or "those people" who are lazy and don't work.

Negative or stereotypical images about residents of public housing impact people's perceptions of the poor and public housing, which gets translated into laws and policies. Public housing laws and policies "assume that it is possible to change the culture in public housing by changing both the physical space and economic mix. The image of community conveyed in the rhetoric of public housing reform presumes that sharing a physical space produces a common culture" (Smith 1999, 2). The council members made it known that despite sharing a physical space, economic hardships (which were tied to other social ills such as mental health and domestic violence), and being in a place where the people are varied culturally, socially, racially, and by age and experience, their "culture" was different from that of the other residents in the community.

The following excerpts from my field notes focus on council members' and residents' conceptions of race and class. Whether anyone would realize it or acknowledge it, race, racial issues, and class dynamics were a concern throughout Rivertown. Trixie (a resident) made a comment about the several cliques that formed and divided community. She said:

> What I see is just like this fine divide and it—people have formed several cliques. They're either friends with people or they're not. They associate with—they won't associate it with this end of the street but they'll only associate with this part of the neighborhood. They don't want to be involved with anybody up on the hill or they don't wanna—you know they, they themselves tell me straight out, "I don't wanna live in that part of the community because I don't like so and so down the street," and I'm like, "That's not a choice and that's not a reason, you know you need to learn to be able to live anywhere and get along."

Terri, one of Rivertown's residents, was scheduled to come to a council meeting to teach participants how to make a wreath. Since the holiday season was soon approaching, the council members thought this project would provide a fun activity in which the whole community might like to be involved. The council members thought that making wreaths would not be expensive and that children could give them away as Christmas gifts. In an effort to publicize the event, the day of the meeting, the council members sent out flyers. When I got to the meeting, however, only Linda, Tiny,[3] and Terri were present—although Tiny was forced to leave soon thereafter (he had undergone chemotherapy earlier in the day). None of the residents in the community showed up. The following excerpt is from my field notes:

> Terri: An older white woman came down to the meeting. She's the craft lady and she brought all this stuff for making wreaths to show all the residents at the community meeting (but no one was there).
>
> For 20 minutes I listened to Terri talk about how she made wreaths and she showed us her big box of supplies and tools. I was very impressed.
>
> What I found out was that Terri had been in Rivertown for a month. She said she used to be a hospice nurse. I never did ask her how she ended up here.
>
> Both ladies were talking about how there was "no sense of community." Hence no one came to this meeting.
>
> Terri said "they" don't care and last Saturday night, she had to call the police on "them." Because "they" were partying until 2:30 a.m. She called the police, then people would go away and a half hour later, "they" would come back.

> She said that some of "these" people live on the hill and "they" drive down to the bottom of the hill. Terri told me that there are a lot of "outsiders" coming into the community.
>
> Then Terri said, she can't relate to "them" unless she gets a "joint and an Icehouse."
>
> She wonders how "they are living" because "they" don't work and "they" sleep all day all and party all night

When I asked Terri who "those people" were, she told me that she meant the younger people who lived in Rivertown, people under the age of twenty-five. As Maynard, the community worker who coordinates a program for the Resolution Action Center (RAC) to work with public housing residents and resident councils, and Vanessa, the Rivertown Manager, pointed out, "older" generally means white while "younger" means urban black. Without overtly stating it, Terri was referring to the young black residents of Rivertown. Both women who were present at this meeting were older and Caucasian.

The bottom of the hill was referred to by residents as "the ghetto." When Linda, the president of the council, first moved into Rivertown, she lived on the bottom of the hill, in the "ghetto" and she had problems with her neighbors. She described the situation:

> My problem was with my neighbors. Down there [lower part of the L]. I was afraid to come out and get into my car if it got kinda dark then I didn't come home. Because I was scared to.
>
> We weren't getting along [African American neighbors] and it was a racial thing going and then my daughter and her daughter [neighbor's daughter] got into a big argument down there and her daughter came out one day and her son said you need to put that shirt over the gun you're carrying in your pocket. And I looked and she had a gun stuck in the back pocket and you know then, my nerves had got just really extremely bad again and I wouldn't come out the house at home.

It's interesting to note that all the council members lived on the top of the hill and no one was from the lower part of the hill (the "ghetto"). As the two only African Americans on the council, Sam and Pebe saw the racial dynamics in the community differently than did the other council members. In an effort to disassociate themselves from the "other" residents in the community, Sam and Pebe both mentioned to me that they were not like those "niggas" in the community. When they used this terminology, they were attributing to other African Americans in the community "negritude traits they disparaged, including tardiness, dishonesty, rudeness, impoverishment, cowardice, and stupidity" (Kennedy 2002, 45). In his book *Nigger: The Strange Career of a Troublesome Word*, Kennedy also maintains that sometimes when blacks use the word "nigga" or "nigger" with reference to other blacks, it is "symptomatic of racial self-hatred" (45) because they have inter-

nalized racial stereotypes. Sam and Pebe made it clear that they were not the
stereotypical black people who lived in public housing. Pebe tried not to act
in the stereotypical way because she thought that to do so meant fewer social
services benefits and resources for her family. She did not want to be discriminated against because of where she lived, the color of her skin, and her
sex. And because Sam considered Rivertown his home, he was offended by
the terminology of the "projects":

> Everybody says the project is the project. When you living here that's your
> home, that's your home. See they gotta like you know like this is "just a
> project" and I says whoa you'll got it mixed up you'll know if you stay here
> two years or three months you got a roof over your head you're blessed and
> that's your home until you go somewhere else. I said you know you all think
> cause it's the project you got to act like the project. It don't work like that
> there.

When I asked Sam why the residents do not join the council, he told me
that in his opinion "they have a negative attitude toward it." When I asked
him why, he said that "the people—the people in general in Rivertown because they didn't want nothing to get up off the ground and work it. They
didn't try to help out. They tried to pull back and hinder every chance we
tried to get going forward."

I also asked Sam about what he thought about people who did not live in
Rivertown, who think that having pretty buildings won't affect people wanting to join the council or even wanting to take pride in where they live. His
response was:

> They got a "nigger's" attitude behind that, because for one reason see they can
> fix their own self. See when I first come in to Rivertown I didn't think I'd stay
> in Rivertown long. But see when I got to here, I always looked at it as my
> home I didn't say it was the projects I looked at it as my home.

Pebe, a mother of three, joined the council to help the children. Even
though she did not know or associate with the parents, she would help out
with the children. Before coming to Rivertown, Pebe and her family had a
house. Economic hard times and her husband's illness put them in Rivertown. Pebe saw herself as different from the other residents in the community. She said to me such things as "Some of those people are beneath me";
"I've seen momma leave their kids for a porch full of niggas"; "They get
checks, food stamps, and live better than me"; and "Half of the people don't
pay rent." Pebe and her husband considered themselves hardworking people,
not like the lazy "niggas" in the community.

Jessica also stereotyped the parents in the community who did not have
jobs. She made it a point to tell her child, that because she cared about her,

she would not let her hang around outside like those other parents who don't care. She said:

> Yeah, the parents pretty much let the kids, most of the parents, just go outside. Most of the time the parents aren't even here. So, I have a hard time with Angie, getting her to realize that I care about her enough not to just go outside and let her do whatever she wants to do. And one day she'll thank me for it. Because a lot of these kids get out here, and I've seen kids get beat up and stuff and nobody's there. I've seen little bitty kids running around in the street.

When I asked her if she thought the parents were working when the children were out, her response was a fast "no."

LIVING IN PUBLIC HOUSING

The term "public housing" has become synonymous with "socio-economic marginalization and behavioral depravity" (Purdy 2003). This small geographical space is represented largely by racial minority populations located in urban centers or inner cities. Several structural and cultural factors such as discrimination, housing policies, and spatial locations have fueled the conception that public housing is exclusively the preserve of "poor minorities" (Macionis and Parrillo 2004, 88). Without question, public housing has a negative reputation.

Despite all the laws and policies that exist to "fix" the negative image and the concentrated effects of poverty—such as the Fair Housing Act of 1965, the Government Performance and Results Act (GPRA) of 1993, and HOPE VI grants—the stigmas and stereotypes still linger. Housing authority officials, managers, community workers, and resident council members are aware of the stigmas and racialized stereotypes that are associated with living in public housing. Even though Rivertown is a diverse community and the majority of the council members are white, issues of race and racial dynamics, class, and the intersections of race and class are prevalent throughout the community.

The next chapter describes the laws and policies that support resident councils and how the housing authority, managers, and communities supported the Rivertown Resident Council's goal of supporting the children in their community. The assumptions the housing authority officials, community workers, and managers have about race, class, and the people in their community inevitably will affect their interactions and involvement with residents.

NOTES

1. I left in most of the "uh," "oh," etc., to retain the original style and speech patterns of the individuals.

2. Pat and Belinda are pseudonyms for Linda's two daughters.

3. Tiny was a member of the resident council. Tiny was also known as the keeper of the keys. If anyone needed to get into the community room after hours, they came to him. Even the children in the community knew he was the key keeper. They may not have known his name but they knew he had those keys. One evening, I went to Rivertown for a meeting. As usual I was early and the door was locked. Several children playing outside the building told me that "the man across the street in that house over there, has keys to the community room." The man to whom they referred was Tiny. Unfortunately, I never got a chance to know Tiny to any great degree or to interview him because he passed away shortly after my arrival to Rivertown.

Chapter Two

Code for Community Engagement

HUD states that the role of the resident council is to engage in community building, provide self-help initiatives, and improve the quality of resident satisfaction. The Rivertown Resident Council planned to achieve such goals by focusing on the children in its community. Focusing on children was a concern that the council members decided was an issue worth pursuing. [1] The children were so important to the resident council that during my time with the council, all of their community-building activities involved children. This chapter focuses on the roles and responsibilities of the resident council as defined by federal laws and regulations. It also explores how the housing authority officials, managers, and community workers interpret these laws and regulations.

THE CODE AND RESIDENT COUNCIL

When I first heard about the resident council, I knew from reading HUD literature and conducting preliminary interviews with the different managers that such bodies played an important role in the structure of public housing. However, at that early stage in my research, I was in the dark regarding the specific function of the council. Over my two years with the council, however, I learned that within the structure of public housing, its role was extremely complex.

Since resident councils are organized in government-funded public housing communities, they must abide by federal rules and regulations established by the *Code of Federal Regulations* (CFR), a codification of all permanent rules and regulations created by federal agencies and executive departments. The CFR is divided into fifty titles that represent broad areas, all of which are subject to federal regulations. For instance, any regulation or law that addresses the subject of education can be found under Title 34; food and drugs, Title 21; protection of the environment, Title 40; housing and urban development, Title 24. Each chapter is divided into parts or sections that cover specific regulatory areas.

Title 24, Section 964.1–964.430 establishes the rules for tenant participation, opportunities in public housing, and the purpose and rules of resident councils in public housing. According to these rules, the housing authorities (HAs) manage the properties and must be in compliance with the CFR. According to the CFR, the council should act to improve the quality of life for its residents and should undertake an active partnership with the HAs to achieve CFR goals. Section 964.100 defines the role of resident councils:

> 964.100. Role of the Resident Council
> The roles of a resident council include improving the quality of life for residents, increasing resident satisfaction, and creating opportunities for self-help initiatives that would enable residents to create for themselves and to their satisfaction a positive living environment. Resident councils may actively participate through a working partnership with the HA to advise and assist in all aspects of public housing operations. (24 C.F.R. 964.100)[2]

Members of the resident council are expected to improve the quality of life and the living environment for all community residents. Tenant concerns are primary, and the purpose of the resident council is to act as the conduit between such concerns and the administration. Section 964.11 HUD Policy on Tenant Participation indicates that

> HUD promotes resident participation and the active involvement of residents in all aspects of a HA's overall mission and operation. Residents have a right to organize and elect a resident council to represent their interests. As long as proper procedures are followed the HA shall recognize the duly elected resident council to participate fully through a working relationship with the HA. HUD encourages HAs and residents to work together to determine the most appropriate ways to foster constructive relationships, particularly through duly-elected resident councils. (24 C.F.R. 964.11)[3]

Under this section, residents have the right to organize to form a resident council that will represent their interests. Section 964.14 HUD Policy on Partnerships emphasizes that a strong partnership with the HAs functions as a crucial component of this endeavor:

> HUD promotes partnerships between residents and HAs which are an essential component to building, strengthening, and improving public housing. Strong partnerships are critical for creating positive changes in lifestyles thus improving the quality of life for public housing residents, and the surrounding community. (24 C.F.R. 964.14)[4]

For example, when I examined the housing authorities' descriptions of resident councils in Philadelphia, Seattle, and Ridgeway, I discovered slightly different interpretations of the roles resident councils should play in their communities. Though different, each housing authority describes the responsibilities and purpose resident councils have toward strengthening and improving their public housing community:

> From the Philadelphia Housing Authority: [5]
> The purpose of each resident council is to identify strategies to improve the quality of life for PHA residents. The Resident Councils serve as advocates for residents and encourage improvements in maintenance and physical conditions, public safety, and support services for residents. Each council helps to plan, implement, monitor, and evaluate the provisions of services, and works with public and private agencies as advocates to obtain additional resources.

> From the Seattle Housing Authority: [6]
> Resident councils generally plan activities and events for their buildings, and also look for ways to make the building friendlier and safer. Sometimes they plan potlucks, social events, and educational events.

> From the Ridgeway Housing Authority:
> In Section 964.100 of the CFR, the Ridgeway Housing Authority, which has authority over Rivertown, provides its own description of resident councils:
> HUD encourages housing authorities and residents to work together to determine the most appropriate methods of fostering constructive relationships, particularly through duly elected resident councils. Each duly elected resident council received individual and group training along with the opportunity to attend seminars and conferences throughout the United States. This training allows residents to network with other public housing residents and housing authority staff members to build new relationships and gain powerful insights on ways to improve their neighborhood. [7]

Legally and theoretically, the *Code of Federal Regulations* gives resident council members—when working in conjunction with the housing authority—some autonomy, support, and resources to improve their communities however they see fit. The policies that guide the council also stress a strong partnership with the housing authority that is designed specifically to help council members reach their community-building goals.

In order to achieve community improvement and self-help initiatives in public housing, while also achieving resident satisfaction and community building within each development, the CFR emphasizes as critical the development of a strong partnership between the resident council and HA. As demonstrated below, managers, housing authority officials, and community workers revealed similar interpretations regarding expectations for the Rivertown Resident Council.

SUPPORTING THE COUNCIL

The Rivertown Resident Council had supportive help like most resident councils in public housing. The managers, housing authority officials, and community workers (who were hired through the housing authority) were there to help the council and members of the community with self-sufficiency and empowerment. The three managers of Rivertown, the housing authority officials, and the community workers agreed and supported the CFR and the role and expectations of the Rivertown Resident Council.

Managers

In the two and a half years I spent studying Rivertown, three managers were assigned to the property: Vanessa, LaTonya, and Dixie. Vanessa managed Rivertown for a total of four years. After Vanessa left, LaTonya managed the community for four months; then Dixie was given the job.

Dixie was a white woman in her midthirties. She was the remarried mother of a little girl and a college graduate from a middle-class background. Her mannerisms reminded me of the comedian Roseanne Barr's—she was up front, loud, and brash. Yet she was also personable and had a great laugh. For instance, when Vanessa and LaTonya would meet with residents or potential residents, they had their office door closed, while other people waited. Dixie, on the other hand, kept her office door wide open. Her ex-husband used to be a policeman, and she had strong ties with the city police. In a year's time, Dixie went from being an office manager, to being trained as a property manager, to actually running four different public housing properties. Dixie stated, "The resident council is here to help the residents to form a better sense of community and to be involved in the community." LaTonya's take on the resident council was "if the residents had concerns or complaints, they could go to the resident council to try to help alleviate some of the issues that were occurring within the community, since they were a governing body of Rivertown."

Sections 964.11 and 964.14 of the CFR establish the importance to community building of the partnership between the resident council and the housing authority. Yet, in their responses, Dixie and LaTonya did not mention as important this relationship. Vanessa also did not mention the resident council as an important link to the housing authority; however, she did define the council as that of "middleman" or liaison between the residents and outside agencies:

> Yeah, it was a big property and a lot of people from other agencies and the community wanted to become involved with Rivertown. And they needed representatives for that site to make decisions about what they would like to have for their community.

Although these managers expressed slightly different interpretations, they all defined the council as helping to build community and as possessing a connection to or link with the residents.

Housing Authority Officials

Of the three housing authority officials I interviewed, only two—Jane and Alvin—possessed job responsibilities that allowed them to have the most direct contact with resident councils. As management director, Daniel described his job responsibility as "oversee[ing] the operations of the Section 8, also the public housing, program." When I asked him what his responsibilities were with resident councils he said:

> Basically for the resident councils the role has changed a bit. I used to be directly related to the resident councils at one time. That's when I had another division called the Community Partnership Division. And in that division, what we did was to actually try to help the residents be more involved at the Ridgeway Housing Authority, talk about maintenance that's being done on that development, improvement, and also try to get them involved in some of the policies that we have written. We also try to help them put in for grants which at one time a couple of the resident councils did receive some grants.
>
> Basically we get monies to get them [resident councils] stipends, you know, each one based on them keeping records of how much money they spend and actually use this money to do programs, to buy specific things for the development that they need.

Because of the restructuring with the housing authority, Daniel told me that "right now, resident councils, most of them are held by a new division that we call the Human Service Division. Along with the Resolution Action Center (RAC) serving as liaison between housing authority and resident councils." Before the arrival of Alvin, Maynard, and Sharon, whose job responsibilities were to work directly with the residents and resident council, Jane was solely responsible for that job task.

For Daniel, the management director of the housing authority, the resident council should function as a tool for self-sufficiency and empowerment. Daniel Harrison was the housing authority's management director, overseeing the operation of all Section 8 housing, as well as the public housing program. He had been involved in such work for over twenty-five years. An African American male in his mid- to late fifties, Daniel was a very tall, stately looking man with short salt-and-pepper hair. He wore glasses and was known for his booming voice. He was the highest-ranking African American in the housing authority.

Despite his rather stately physical appearance, Daniel was very laid back, humorous, and personable. At joint resident council meetings, I watched him work the room like a good politician, smiling, laughing, shaking hands.

Compared to the other housing authority officials with whom I have interacted, he was the most outgoing. In Daniel's estimation, the role the resident
council plays in establishing self-sufficiency can be drawn directly from CFR
964.100 Role of Resident Council, which stresses that the council should
"participate in self-help initiative[s]." In Daniel's view,

> There's a need for a resident council. I mean, you have people on develop-
> ments who have input in what's going on. I mean, it's their lives too. And
> we're talking about upward mobility. And they need to be involved in things
> that will enhance their awareness of things that they need to do and things they
> can do to help themselves and help other people. It's a community. . . . Their
> responsibility is to try to make themselves become self-sufficient. Or, if not, to
> help other people become self-sufficient.

The connection between the council and the community was made by
Alvin, the neighborhood coordinator with the housing authority. He reiterat-
ed the theme that the resident council spoke for the residents. He said that the
purpose of the resident council "was to have one voice speaking on behalf of
the residents within that given community and to develop a partnership with
the housing authority." Alvin further indicated that the resident council "is
supposed to be anything that our residents have a concern about, which can
be good, but many times it's something where they have a concern about
either the way we're providing a service, a service that they think should be
provided, or about an expectation that has not been met." Alvin Miller is a
thirty-something, African American male who has been working for the
housing authority for less than a year. Originally from New York, he has a
background in social services. Before he came to the housing authority, he
was a food stamp eligibility worker with the City of Ridgeway. Not only
does he work for the housing authority, but he is also a married father of two
and a church deacon.

Community Workers

Maynard and Sharon were a married couple in their late twenties and early
thirties from New Orleans, Louisiana. I call them Afrocentric hippies because they had truly immersed themselves in the history, knowledge, drum-
ming, and dancing of African culture. Both were vegetarians (as were their
two dogs) and Muslims. They had incorporated African-centered traditions
into their extremely successful workshops, outreach, and community-building activities for the adults and children in the public housing communities.
    Sharon wore her hair natural, in braids or a twist, and was fond of vividly
colored flowing clothes and hair wraps. Maynard wore Afrocentric jewelry
and attire. They liked to hike, fish, canoe, and mountain climb. Maynard was
taking classes to be a certified scuba diver.

Since they were always together they jokingly told people to just call them "Shamayne." Shamayne came to the state from New Orleans five years ago because they had exhausted their resources in that Louisiana city, and they needed a positive change. In New Orleans, the couple ran into economic hard times. They were working odd jobs; when they could find work, they couldn't afford a car, phone, or a decent place to live. One day they found a bike that someone threw out, and, after Maynard fixed it, it became a primary mode of transportation (in addition to public transit). They lived in a high-crime neighborhood, in a place also occupied by bugs and rodents. They were down on their luck and had gotten tired of having to constantly borrow money from family and friends. Eventually, parents and friends cut them off because they had borrowed so much.

One day, Sharon got a message from her cousin, who was living in the state where this research takes place, asking the couple to visit. They borrowed a truck and drove fifteen hours. Once in the state, they said, "we loved it and it felt right, it felt good." Three weeks later they made a permanent move and started looking for work. One day Sharon found an ad in the newspaper for a program trainer/mediator who would help public housing residents overcome conflict. Once she had the job, Maynard would volunteer and help her out. Soon after, he became a program coordinator for residents and resident organizations in public housing.

Sharon echoed the views of Daniel, Jane, and Alvin when she stated her opinion that the purpose of the Rivertown council is "to empower the residents in the community . . . [a]nd they are a liaison between the residents and the housing authority to bring programs and different benefits to the community." Maynard had a simple ten-word description of the role of the resident council. He said, "It's the job of the council to empower the community."

Overall, the managers, housing authority officials, and community workers defined the purpose of the council as helping build community and assisting the residents, whether through empowerment, the teaching of self-sufficiency, being a liaison between the housing authority and the residents, or being the representative for resident concerns and issues.

Both Jane's and Alvin's interpretation of the council overlapped. To them, the council represented the voice and the concerns of the community, which were then relayed to the housing authority. In other words, the council served as the communication link between the housing authority and residents. Alvin was the only person to mention the council as "developing a partnership with the housing authority," which is a goal stated in 964.11 and 964.14 of the CFR. For Daniel, the primary goal of the council should be helping residents with self-sufficiency.

RESPONSIBILITIES FOR COMMUNITY SUCCESS

The housing authority officials, community workers, and managers[8] under-stood the role(s) of resident councils in public housing communities. Hous-ing authority officials, community workers, and managers identified several specific job responsibilities and duties of the resident council that helped its members achieve a positive living environment for their community and build a strong partnership with the housing authority. These individuals also articulated their responsibilities to the council.

Jane, the former resident council coordinator with the housing authority, said she "was responsible for ensuring that each neighborhood had a properly elected resident council that represented the needs of the residents to the housing authority and would effectively relay requests or decisions from the housing authority to the residents in the neighborhood. We were kind of like a communication bridge." Jane would go to all the resident council members in all the public housing communities and help them organize, plan events, and follow the CFR rules for proper election of resident councils. Jane Ad-ams, a white woman in her late fifties, was a former nun who held a master's degree in education. Before joining the housing authority, she worked as a volunteer coordinator for nonprofit local ministries and soup kitchens. Jane first started working for the housing authority in 1995, when she was hired as a resident council coordinator, a position she left. Because of organizational restructuring, Alvin, Maynard, and Sharon now did the job that Jane once did by herself.

Alvin Miller, the neighborhood coordinator, described his responsibility as "primarily to work with each of our communities as it relates to, not only the resident councils, but any services that can be provided that are currently not being provided in any of those communities." When I asked him about his specific responsibility with the council, he told me that it involved edu-cating and promoting the resident council to the residents:

> It's our responsibility to begin conversations to, number one, educate the peo-ple over there that they should have a resident council. Then after we do that, it's our job to educate the residents on what the resident council is all about. One of the things that I use the resident council for quite often is to let them know about all of the partnerships that we have.

Alvin also saw his responsibility as that of a link between the council and outside opportunities, a position that involved informing the resident coun-cils about numerous partnerships available to help them achieve their goals.

Community Workers

Similarly, community workers interacted with the council and thus bore responsibility toward it. For example, Maynard coordinated a program for the Resolution Action Center (RAC), a capacity-building program funded by HUD for residents and resident organizations in public housing, and he defined his role as helping the council get organized and build skills. Maynard was so passionate about his role that he hoped eventually it would be eliminated—that one day the need for it would no longer exist. Describing his responsibilities, Maynard said:

> I am primarily focused on working with getting the resident councils organized and trying to get them the skills, or offer them the skills, that would make them more effective. So, basically, my role and purpose is to develop them to the point where a Maynard Assuliman, or whoever at the housing authority, is not a necessity. They are only a luxury. So that whenever they want to do something, they know how to do it, they know who to go to, and how to make it happen.

He continued his description:

> My job is to empower the resident council so they can empower their community. I am not going to go through Rivertown knocking on doors explaining what the resident council is about. I will explain to the resident council if they don't know what they're about. What their overall objective and mission should be.

As a part of his job, Maynard was required to make council members fully aware of pertinent laws and policies that govern and shape their actions and rights. As he explained, "Many of the councils are not aware of their rights as a council. They're not aware of the *Code of Federal Regulations* that governs the councils, and also governs the housing authority and the relationship between the two of them. So I work with both the housing authority and councils as a middleman between both of them to try to build the bridge of respect and working together so that they can become more effective. Both of them."

Maynard defined his responsibility to the resident council in Ridgeway as that of a bridge, a communication link between the council members and the housing authority. By informing the residents about the CFR and their rights, he hoped to give them the tools to empower themselves and the community. Whereas Alvin worked with the resident council and the residents, Maynard worked solely with the resident council.

Sharon, a program coordinator with RAC, ran a HUD-funded program called Resolutions, in which she taught residents how to overcome conflict without using violence. Describing her position, she said, "I have a program called Resolutions which is in all the neighborhoods for the Ridgeway Housing Authority and basically I'm a trainer/mediator for the communities and I basically train residents um on how to overcome conflict without fighting with each other and violence and all that stuff. Basically, how to deal with one another without conflict." Sharon worked specifically with the residents and the resident councils in public housing. Comparing her responsibilities with those of Maynard in regard to the resident councils, she said, "I'm neutral, because I'm a mediator, um, but the capacity-building coordinator is more of an advocate for the resident councils, and that's Maynard Assuliman, so he's not a neutral party." Levels of neutrality aside, the mere act of interaction and how the community workers interpret laws and policies meant that community workers in some way influenced the council. Likewise, managers—always on the front lines in public housing communities—worked closely with the council.

All the housing authority officials agreed with the CFR and the purpose and goals of a resident council in public housing. Jane, Alvin, Maynard, Sharon, and the managers all realized their job responsibilities to help the council to become successful. To be successful meant helping the council organize, plan, and understand the laws and policies that govern the council.

Not Meeting Expectations

There are numerous laws and policies in public housing that support and encourage resident councils to build community. The laws and policies establish the rules and responsibilities of the council, stress the critical relationship between the housing authority and resident council, and articulate the importance and structure of resident council relationships.

From the interpretations of the laws and policies provided by the housing authority officials, managers, and community workers, it is clear that they understood not only the necessity for implementing and enforcing these policies in order to enhance the council but also the importance they played collectively in helping the council improve their community and become self-sufficient.

Even through the HUD officials[9] followed and supported the CFR to support and enhance the council, in the end they did not think the resident council members were meeting expectations because the individuals on the council (1) lacked leadership, (2) had communication issues, (3) did not take advantage of the support and resources that HUD offered, and (4) operated under laws and policies that could be described as problematic. On the other hand, resident council members believed that they were working toward their goal of improving the lives of children in the community, but they argued that housing authority officials, managers, and community workers ignored their responsibilities, failed to attend meetings, and did not explain the CFR and other housing laws and regulations with clarity. Clearly, disjunctions exist. These disjunctions were sometimes obstacles that the resident council could not overcome.

NOTES

1. As Alvin stated, "The resident council is supposed to be anything that our residents have a concern about." Depending on the location, situation, and needs of the public housing communities, the focus can vary, from improving safety or conditions of the elderly, to eradicating crime, improving resources, and so forth.

2. Housing and Urban Development, *Code of Federal Regulations*, title 24(2010): Part 964 Tenant Participation and Tenant Opportunities in Public Housing, chapter IX: Office of Assistant Secretary for Public and Indian Housing, Department of Housing and Urban Development (Parts 901–1699), accessed March 5, 2015, http://www.gpo.gov/fdsys/browse/collectionCfr. action?collectionCode=CFR&searchPath=Title+24%2FSubtitle+B%2FChapter+Ix&oldPath= Title+24%2FSubtitle+B&isCollapsed=true&selectedYearFrom=2010&ycord=1167.

3. Housing and Urban Development, *Code of Federal Regulations*, title 24(2010): Part 964 Tenant Participation and Tenant Opportunities in Public Housing, chapter IX: Office of Assistant Secretary for Public and Indian Housing, Department of Housing and Urban Development (Parts 901–1699), accessed March 5, 2015, http://www.gpo.gov/fdsys/browse/collectionCfr. action?collectionCode=CFR&searchPath=Title+24%2FSubtitle+B%2FChapter+Ix&oldPath= Title+24%2FSubtitle+B&isCollapsed=true&selectedYearFrom=2010&ycord=1167.

4. Housing and Urban Development, *Code of Federal Regulations*, title 24(2010): Part 964 Tenant Participation and Tenant Opportunities in Public Housing, chapter IX: Office of Assistant Secretary for Public and Indian Housing, Department of Housing and Urban Development (Parts 901–1699), accessed March 5, 2015, http://www.gpo.gov/fdsys/browse/collectionCfr. action?collectionCode=CFR&searchPath=Title+24%2FSubtitle+B%2FChapter+Ix&oldPath= Title+24%2FSubtitle+B&isCollapsed=true&selectedYearFrom=2010&ycord=1167.

5. "Philadelphia Housing Authority," last modified February 25, 2015, http://www.pha. phila.gov/.

6. "Tenant Information," *Seattle Housing Authority*, last modified February 25, 2015, http://www.seattlehousing.org/residents/information/.

7. Managers' responsibilities and the dynamic relationship between the resident council and the manager will be its own separate section.

8. After Jane left the housing authority, Alvin was hired under the Human Service Division. Now Alvin, Maynard, and Sharon work together toward resident satisfaction. Before the restructuring, Jane was a one-woman army. Her job was to specifically deal with the resident councils.

9. HUD officials include Ridgeway Housing Authority officials, managers, and community workers.

Chapter Three

Who's Leading the Council?

When I first asked the community workers, housing authority officials, and managers why the Rivertown Resident Council was not effective, why they were not the active agents for community change that HUD and HA had envisioned, a common response focused on "lack of leadership" and "laziness." All the council members interpreted the primary purpose of the Rivertown Council to be helping the children in Rivertown, with a secondary purpose geared toward helping the community as a whole.

INTERPRETING THE ROLE OF THE COUNCIL

Laziness and Lack of Leadership

Many of the housing authorities' officials thought that focusing on children was a cop-out. They should be doing more. At the same time their expectations were not what the council members had. Both Maynard and Sharon felt that fear was preventing a strong leadership from developing within the Rivertown Council. Maynard stated that a strong leader was needed for the council, a person who would not be afraid of or back down from real issues:

> They need a strong leader, you know, someone who is going to . . . whenever we, in any of the communities we deal with, whenever there's a controversial subject that comes up in the community all the residents come out, the room is packed, you've got to borrow seats to fill the room up, so you need someone that's going to keep . . . when all the feathers get ruffled, and I'm not saying someone antagonistic, but you need someone that's going to address the real issues and that's not afraid to address the real issues in the community.

Maynard also expressed his belief that lack of a strong leader was related to individual motivation and that the lack of individual motivation could lead to failures of policy and assistance. The agency, he noted, was doing all it could:

> And that's because . . . well, no, because the housing authority held a meeting in each neighborhood, informing them of all these things, so it all boils down to the individual and what they want; you can't blame the housing authority for that and you can't blame the government for that, you gotta blame the individual for not getting off their backside and actually wanting to do something.

If a stronger leader was someone unafraid of getting involved and dealing with issues in the community, then Sharon also suggested that fear was preventing leadership from arising in the Rivertown Council. "Rivertown I know has had a pretty rough time establishing a resident council, a strong resident council, um, since I've been in this position," she said. "I think from my observations many of the residents on the council are afraid to get out into the community and, um, really aggressively work the community."

Maynard and Sharon interpreted the council as weak—not having motivation or a strong leader, or possessing leadership qualities among its various members. Despite community dynamics or personal issues, they both felt the council could overcome those deficits and work to become a strong force in the community.

The last manager, Dixie, resonated a similar feeling. Dixie attempted to show her support by letting the council handle their own business without involvement or interference from the manager. In her words, "They need to handle their residents, so to speak, at their own level."

Dixie also expressed her opinions that the individual bore the responsibility of providing for himself or herself and that if the council members were forced to handle their own business, they simply could not be lazy. Dixie said:

> I think a lot of it boils down to—I hate to say it, but laziness because they find out they actually have to go do something now and then and they just don't want to be bothered. They want somebody to do it for them and then they just want to reap the benefits and you know unfortunately I think they're going to have a shock when the community service things are really hard-core implemented and they need to uphold those and they've not complied and they're being evicted for it, so. . .

If the council members needed her help or suggestion, however, Dixie was there, although she seemed to prefer a "hands-off" approach. As a manager, she saw her primary role as dealing with management issues.

Linda the Council Leader

The council did have a leader, a strong one, Linda. While the Rivertown Council did not officially elect officers to the council—instead opting for a more egalitarian setup—Linda often performed the multiple and time-consuming duties of an elected president. She said that she would

> keep all the records of everything and, kept the checks and I more or less did most of things on my own. When Tiny [a council member that passed away] was around he helped a lot and then Alvin just said, "Whatever you want to do." So it was pretty much up to me. I did the shopping for the events and carried out the events to make sure everything went okay and, made sure that every meeting that I could I would attend, or try to make sure that somebody else attended.

Jessica saw Linda as the individual who was capable of enacting the sort of positive leadership model that would enable the council to work on its own. As she indicated, "Ms. Linda was the one that pulled everything together pretty much." In Sam's terms, "Linda gets things organized and together." In fact, I have witnessed this; if Linda was absent from a meeting, it inevitably tended to fall apart and not be as organized as when she was present. She was capable of getting the council together and keeping its members motivated.

Under Linda's leadership the council had several activities for children in the community. What needs to be examined are the community dynamics, who's running the council meetings, and the roles and expectations of the housing authority officials. Part of the "assumption" of laziness and lack of leadership goes to the confusion of the roles and responsibilities of the HA officials to the resident council members. According to the CFR and HUD regulations, resident councils were created to empower public housing residents—to, in effect, give them some autonomy, control, and leadership of their community. According to these regulations, the role of the housing authority officials is to support the council, not manage it or dictate its goals.

Yet, Jane and Vanessa thought the leader of the council should be the manager. Vanessa tended to extend her support in a different manner, defining her responsibility as that of "bringing the council together." Both Vanessa and Jane believed the manager should be the leader of the resident council. Vanessa even defined this as her responsibility. She said, "I had a very good Rivertown Resident Council. The residents in Rivertown, just like residents that I got together at all the other councils and properties, are people that need their property manager to be their leader. Plain and simple. They need a leader just like any other organization." Vanessa was the manager at Rivertown for four years—the first African American and the first woman to be property manager. She was a single mother of two boys and had been with the housing authority for over ten years. In her thirties she got married, had two boys, and then was divorced. Her ex-husband became involved in illegal activities and was currently in jail. As she described the situation:

> He used to have a nice auto repair business, but he started taking people's money and not finishing the job. He was doing crack and he had started drinking.

Her husband's drinking and drug use only escalated the physical and mental abuse that she received from him.

When it came to managing Rivertown, Vanessa possessed a skill that amazed me. She knew the names of all residents, as well as detailed information about them, and she could tell you the numbers of the apartments in which they lived. To some degree, she acted as a therapist for residents, who frequently came to talk with her about situations that were going on in their lives and in the neighborhood. For example, residents came to Vanessa when a teenage girl (eighteen years old) in Rivertown was having oral sex in the Laundromat where everybody could witness it. Then, later on, Vanessa got a call from the maintenance man, who told her that the same girl's toilet was clogged because it was filled with condoms. Vanessa went over to the apartment and told the girl how to properly dispose of condoms and how to conduct herself in a ladylike manner and to be safe.

The fact that Vanessa was very people oriented could be witnessed by her eventual pursuit of a master's degree in social work. When new applicants moved into Rivertown, Vanessa would tell them about the council and why they should be involved. She was always present at council meetings and at community events.

Despite the fact that the CFR states that resident council members should lead their own organizations, even among the managers, community workers, and housing authority officials there was some confusion with regard to who was responsible for leading the council. Since various individuals on all levels articulated differing conceptions of leadership, it is little wonder that the council itself was hampered by leadership issues.

Jane provided a mechanism by which the council could take advantage of a strong leader already available to them: she believed that the resident manager should lead the council. In Jane's view, having a manager as the leader simply made things easier: "Just let the manager decide to and let somebody who's there from eight in the morning until five in the afternoon on a good day uh and not there on the weekends not there at night . . . that person run it [the resident council]."

In public housing, residents move in and out on a regular basis as their fortunes improve or destabilize, so transience can affect the council, as well as community leadership in general. Jane expressed a belief that since managers were around more often, they could provide the stable and strong leadership vital to ongoing projects and long-term goals. According to Jane, the individuals who, because of emotional stability and positive personalities, are best suited for leadership positions on the council are also those who are least likely to live for very long in the housing projects. Jane put it this way:

> Another problem that the people who generally express an interest in being on a resident council usually have—they're not the depressed people. They're not the—they have, they have some pizzazz. They tend to be the people who are gonna move on fairly quickly. They have some leadership, some and it may be misdirected um now but um if you get a good resident council going chances are those folks aren't going to be there very, very long.

Linda and the other council members were not "depressed" people. Linda may be chronically depressed but she was able to function, plan, and organize meetings and activities for the council. She was able to do so despite the managers trying to "run the council." Members of the council agreed that, in terms of her people skills, Vanessa was a successful manager who was always willing to help them with personal problems and lend a sympathetic ear. When it came to the Resident Council, however, she was far less effective. Defining the manager's responsibilities to the council, Sam stated that "she had nothing to do with the council." In Sam's view, when Vanessa managed Rivertown, nothing was accomplished in the community. He reported that "things I was telling Vanessa wasn't done."

FOCUS ON THE CHILDREN

The resident council's emphasis on children was one of the major areas of disjunction between its members and community workers. The council members wanted their activities to be children centered, but the community workers and housing authority officials conceived of a far different focus for the council. For example, Maynard believed the council should move beyond its focus on children. He saw the council as a resource for tackling major issues in the community, not just those related to children:

> Well, in communities where I hear "Let's focus on the kids," is because the adults don't want to deal with adults. The children are easy to control. The children don't bring the issues that adults bring. But really if you deal with the adults you are helping the children. If you deal with the adults, you are benefiting the kids. . . . But with me right now dealing with the adults, there's far more success in those communities than when I was just dealing with the children. But in some communities the parents don't want to get involved, so that's who you're left to deal with is the children. And that may be what the

> Rivertown Council has found, that you can't get the parents involved. So they
> have to deal with the children.

In spite of Maynard's implication that the resident council focused on children because adults would not attend activities, the resident council's focus was consistent with a need identified by Krivo and Peterson (1996). They note that in poor communities there were few community-based institutions to supervise youth activities. Further, "families, neighbors, and other primary groups" were less likely to interact with youth in-group activities (622). They argue that the lack of community and institutional involvement with youth increases the likelihood of delinquency and crime. The resident council's activities for the community's young people could be interpreted as rudimentary delinquency-prevention programs.

Focusing on "just the kids" is a complex issue. The council members had on numerous occasions attempted to involve parents in activities for their children, but they experienced little or no success. For example, the council members held several meetings to consider planning a summer trip for the children. They planned on taking them to a state amusement park, Kings Island, four hours from the city of Ridgeway. Council members had worked with the housing authority and received funding for transportation, lodging, and admission fees into the park. Of the parents, they asked only three things: that they volunteer to help plan the activity, chaperone the trip, and pay $15 to help fund the venture. As Sam later told me, "We couldn't get the parents to volunteer to help out. Like, you know, we would give some money to help out and they didn't want to give their share to, you know, pitch in to help out and make [the plan] more feasible. . . . They wanted us to support the whole load. See, we were going to volunteer to give $500 toward Kings Island and they [would] pay like $15 per child themselves. They didn't want to do that. They wanted us to take on the whole thing and chaperone the kids, too, and that was too much." Since this would have been a weekend trip, it might have been difficult for parents to take off work or even find the monies to pay $15 for their children to go on this trip. Sam might have lost sight of the fact that parent(s) were working two to three jobs or have a limited income. So they might not have had the finances or time.

At the time of planning the trip there were four active council members: Sam, Linda, Tiny, and Pebe. Tiny would not have been able to go on the trip because of his chemotherapy. That would have left Sam and Linda (both of whom are in their fifties) and Pebe (who was in her late twenties) to watch between twenty and thirty-five kids. Without question, they needed physical help in addition to the support, funding, and partnership they received from the manager and the housing authority. The failed Kings Island trip represents just one example of the difficulties the council faced when it attempted to involve parents in its activities for children. In fact, when activities were planned for children in the community, it was the children themselves, rather than the parents, who most often volunteered to help. This event demonstrated leadership and being pro-action, not laziness.

ENFORCEMENT AND IMPLEMENTATIONS OF POLICIES

Another area of disjunction entwined with the council's focus on children was the enforcement and implementation of housing policies. Since Alvin also believed the resident council's focus should move beyond just children, policies were created to enforce his "difference in focus of the resident council." Alvin believed Rivertown Council's primary roles should involve informing the manager about illegal activities, improving the neighborhood, and reporting lease violations. According to Alvin, "if people come to a meeting and they say apartment 305 is selling drugs and it happens between eleven p.m. and three a.m., yes, the resident council is going to take that information to the manager. Now the persons that are in that apartment, will they perceive the resident council as snitch?[1] Oh sure. And it comes up in many of our communities. But that's [just] one of those things if the resident council is to improve the neighborhood." Alvin also indicated his belief that the council should focus some of its attention on preventing lease violations:

> And if there's somebody violating their lease, it's up to the resident council, if they have that information, to share it. Not accuse, but to share what they've been told and to go from there. And that is one of the most difficult things of why some people choose not to belong to the resident council, because that's what they perceive as their job. And that's only one small part. But it is about a relationship because we don't want anyone in our communities, if someone is selling drugs or doing something that they shouldn't be doing. Someone living in an apartment and they're not on the lease. Those are some of the things that the council has to deal with.

However, HUD rules do not state that it is mandatory for councils to report lease violations and police the community, unless its members *want* to. Moreover, neither the CFR nor the Ridgeway Housing Authority mission and operations statement states that resident councils must report lease violations and police their communities. Although one can interpret that in their focus on improving the neighborhood the policies of the CFR and the Ridgeway Housing Authority encompass having the council serve as a police agent; after all, the specific methods by which resident council members achieve community improvement are not dictated specifically by any law. However, Rivertown Council members did not define their role(s) to be that of *policeman* or *authority*, although other resident councils had incorporated "community policing and safety" into their purpose statements. Instead, Riv-

ertown's council members made it clear that the community's children would
be the vehicles by which they worked to achieve community improvement.
Since Alvin developed his own definition of the Rivertown Resident Council's purpose, his focus differed from theirs and resulted in a breakdown in
cooperation.

In short, when he perceived the role of the council to encompass policing
the development, Alvin did not fully comprehend or consider community
dynamics. The emotional backlash council members could have confronted
and the potentially physical threats they could have faced as a result of
reporting lease violations and illegal activities made the role of policing their
community unwise. Besides, reporting and dealing with lease violations was
the manager's responsibility—not something for which council members
were held accountable. Managers were fully aware of such responsibility.
When I asked the three managers of Rivertown to describe their managerial
duties, Dixie said, "To make sure people aren't in violation of their lease";
LaTonya said, "I was responsible for the full property management of the
property"; and Vanessa said she was "responsible for lease violations."

If it was the manager's job to report lease violations and Alvin thought
that reporting lease violations was something the resident council should do,
then his focus differed from that of the council members. Alvin did not even
consider the laws involving lease violations or the repercussions that council
members could face if they take on the roles of police agents. There are
specific CFR laws, supported by the Supreme Court, which address lease
violations in public housing. The Supreme Court ruling in *Rucker v. Davis*
(1998) solidified HUD's policy on lease violations. In 2002, the U.S. Supreme Court sided with the Oakland Housing Authority (OHA) and its zero
tolerance eviction policy, which allows for eviction of public housing tenants
if relatives or visitors are caught with drugs on the premises or other public
properties even if the tenants in question did not know about the illegal
activity.[2] This case involved Danielle Rucker, a sixty-three-year-old grandmother who lived with her daughter, two grandchildren, and a great-grand-
daughter in public housing in Oakland, California. Her daughter was caught
with cocaine three blocks away from their home, while her son, who did not
live with her, was caught using cocaine eight blocks from her home. Rucker
had no idea about her children's drug usage, but regardless of this fact she
was evicted. According to this ruling, any drug activity in the home or near
the home will lead to tenant eviction, a policy indicated by Title 24, Subsec-
tion 966, which addresses "Dwelling, Leases, Procedures, and Requirements." According to this policy, OHA includes in its leases the obligation
that a tenant must ensure that any member of the household or another person
under the tenant's control shall not engage in (i) Any criminal activity that
threatens the health, safety, or right to peaceful enjoyment of the premises by
other public housing residents or threatens the health and safety of the hous-

ing authority employees . . . or (ii) Any drug-related criminal activity on or near the premises (e.g., manufacture, sale, distribution, use, or possession of illegal drugs or drug paraphernalia, etc.) (24 C.F.R. 966).

In the Rucker case, there were several senior citizens who, as leaseholders, were evicted from their apartments because the children or grandchildren with whom they lived sold or used drugs. For residents of public housing, such a policy holds dire consequences. According to the 1997 U.S. Census Bureau, 3.9 million grandparents are raising their grandchildren (Glass and Huneycutt 2002). In 2000, a quarter of a million of those grandparent-caregivers were living below the poverty line (Fuller-Thomson and Minkler 2003). In Rivertown, too, twenty elderly residents live with their children and/or grandchildren.

The example of *Rucker v. Davis* (1998) is used here to illustrate the difficulties that would be inherent in demanding that council members assume the responsibility of reporting lease violations or illegal activities. Rivertown was a community of strong personal relationships. Residents were known to one another. Reporting a violation could cause a friend or someone the council knew who was elderly, poor, or ill to be evicted from his or her home and the grandchildren that that individual cared for to be displaced. Hence, if they were expected to act as "police," resident council members faced a double bind: by reporting violations, they knowingly bore responsibility for destroying someone's home, even if the person in question was not engaging in illegal activity, and in doing so they likewise became "snitches" who turned on their neighbors, the very individuals they were elected to help.

Additionally, there is no getting around the fact that reporting lease violations or illegal activities involves the real threat of danger to council members. For instance, one night Linda called the police about a domestic violence situation in the community, and within a short amount of time the word was out that she had reported the incident. The next day, she found sixteen nails driven into one of her car tires.

Obviously, Alvin's focus extended beyond what the council itself wanted to do. But the matter does not end there. Since Alvin's conception of the council's focus was different, his expectations of the roles and responsibilities its members should adopt also differed. Given that Alvin thought the role of the council should be to report lease violations and police the community, then his conception of their responsibilities might not have involved any children-centered activities or programs. So there was a disjunction between the council's chosen focus on children and external demands that they focus on enforcement and implementation of policies. As a result, Alvin's evaluation of the council could be tainted by his assumption that they "shirked" their real duties to plan programs for children. To reiterate, according to policy, housing authority officials are supposed to do their best to create the sort of strong partnership with council members that will help the latter achieve their goal, however they define it. In fact, each person involved with the resident council had a specific responsibility for helping the group achieve its goal. If housing authority officials and community workers differed in their opinion regarding what the resident council should do, then they would also differ with regard to the activities they expected its members to undertake.

SNITCHING

Alvin brought up the issue of snitching, which was another area of disjunction. Snitching (even the perception of it) not only put the resident council members at risk, but it affected the ability of the resident council to recruit new members and have residents actively participate in the community. In spite of the activities, funding, and advertising of the council, the resident council was perceived by some in the community as negative rather than positive. Notions of negativity stemmed from the recruitment practices of the manager, the relationship between the manager and the residents, and the rules and federal policies by which the residents had to abide,[3] which states what they could or could not do and who they could or could not have living with or visiting them.

Sharon realized that if one was on the resident council one would be perceived as being the manager's pet. Hence, that may be why residents were afraid to join the council. She said:

> Um, I think that many of them don't want to be seen as ah "Ridgeway Housing Authority pets" you know [*laughs*]. I think they're afraid that their neighbors may look at them as snitches or you know somebody that's watching them all the time so they just don't want to get involved in it.

To verify this assumption regarding public response, manager Vanessa related a story about a woman who was on the council but resigned after being labeled a snitch. At the time, Vanessa couldn't understand what the fuss was about since participation on the council was strictly voluntary rather than paid. She attributed the false perception of council members as snitches to simple ignorance of the group's role. She said:

> Sometimes being on the resident council in public housing, you get labeled. As a resident you get labeled, labeled as a snitch. Labeled as somebody telling all the business of other neighbors.

Several of the resident council members spoke forthrightly about how being on the council got them labeled as snitches. While talking to one of the residents in the community, for example, Jessica found out firsthand what the residents thought about the council. She said:

> I don't know, just talkin' to some of the residents here, with them not knowing I was on the council and for them to sit there and say that, you know . . . I was talkin' to somebody and they didn't know I was on the council. I guess because there wasn't an election and I haven't talked to many of the residents around here, not that many people knew. So they were just talkin' about how they felt that resident council was a snitch and just a gossip session and all we're there for is just to look out and be nosey and run back to the property manager.

In Jessica's opinion, the fear of "snitching" and of being labeled a snitch prevented many individuals from volunteering to assume positions on the council. She expressed her belief that the council wanted to do a lot of things but couldn't get help for that simple reason. She said:

> Well, they [resident council members] meant well and they wanted to do a lot more than what actually got done. There just wasn't enough help there from the community, volunteers, and stuff. I just think a lot of the people out here think that being on the council and helpin' them do stuff, they're considered snitches and they think of the council as people who are nosey and they go back and tell the landlord what's going on around here.

When the council did attract new members, they tended not to stay very long. Linda told me how one of Jessica's friends moved into Rivertown and was initially excited about being on the council and helping out. After talking to the residents in the community, however, she changed her mind. Linda said:

> I don't have any ideas on how to do it [change the image of the council as a snitch] because Jessica's neighbor . . . a friend moved in down there. I don't know if she's still down there or not. But, anyway, before she got moved in she told me she'd be on the council. So when she got moved in, then she came up here and was talking to us and said, "Well, I decided I don't want to be on the council. It's too much hassle and I don't want people mad at me." See, if you're on the council here, you're an automatic snitch.

Like Vanessa, Sam thought the residents were ill informed for thinking that all the council members do was gossip to the manager. He said:

> I think it's like this here they are dumb to the fact that you know if they come down here and set in on a meeting—if they can give—like we come in here from an hour if they can give us an hour of their time and we sat in here and explained to 'em what they be doing I think they'd have more understanding. . . .

> Well like I think the um the people we had on there and the residents down
> in Rivertown they thought that the peoples on the resident council was going
> back and telling—going on to the ah managers . . . yeah, it wasn't like that.

In an attempt to explain why the community thought the council members
were snitches, Sam offered the simple verdict that people often had a guilty
conscience. He noted:

> People have got a guilty conscience themselves, see. It's as simple as that. If
> they got a guilty conscience they gonna have to blame somebody, and so I
> guess what they did see they blamed somebody else see then the residents we
> had on the council they get in and argue with the kids and stuff like that there
> and they end up quitting.

There is something to be said about the "guilty conscience." Because the
housing authority and HUD have strict leasing rules regarding pets, guests,
and employment (the more money a person makes, the higher that person's
rent will be), a lot of rules get broken in secret. And there are a lot of rules to
break. For instance, the June 2003 *Public Housing Occupancy Guidebook*
(HUD 2003b) offers over two hundred pages detailing rules and information
for living in federal housing, such as income rents, qualifications for admis-
sions for living in public housing, civil rights and nondiscrimination requirements, occupancy guidelines, community service and economic self-sufficiency, domestic violence, and grievance procedures. The thirteen-page lease
that residents have to sign gives further detail about what residents can and
cannot do and defines the punishments that will be imposed if they violate
any of the rules. For instance, if unsatisfactory housekeeping conditions are
reported to the housing authority, the manager will inspect the apartment. If
the problem is not resolved, the resident will be given written notice of the
violations, which must be corrected within twenty-one days. If after a second
inspection the violation is not corrected, the tenant will be issued a thirty-day
moving notice. Or if a tenant wishes to have a "guest" stay longer than
fourteen days, he or she must receive permission from the housing authority.
The housing authority has strict rules in its lease about household composition, what constitutes a guest, covered person, or other person under the
tenant's control.

Since adherence to the rules became a crucial component of being allowed to remain in public housing, residents in violation were often fearful
and distrustful—and they often lashed out against resident council members
who had done nothing. For example, when Linda's neighbor had an illegal
number of people living with her, she confronted Linda, who she thought
was "snitching on her." Linda said:

Well, you talk to somebody, when it gets back to you it's five times different than what you said, and they're the only person you said it to, so you know they said it to begin with, or the other person wouldn't know it. And then it's just made up into a big tale that I told. And so just don't talk to me no more. Phyllis [a resident of Rivertown] come runnin' up here and asked me why I went down to the office to tell that her daughter was living there. And I said, "Look, you having 14 people in your house doesn't bother my household at all. I don't care if you've got 25 in there. I really don't care." And I said, "I'm not on the council anymore. I'm not tellin' nothing so y'all can just shut your mouths and just leave me alone."

Because of the changes in management and the overarching rules and regulations that residents had to adhere to, getting chummy with the manager was perceived as snitching. That the resident council members did not want to be perceived as snitches by the community's residents is consistent with the larger literature on snitching, whistle-blowing, and "codes of silence." Once a group or individual is labeled as a snitch or tattletale, they lose the respect of their peers (Rosenfeld, Jacobs, and Wright 2003). Thus, the pressure put on the resident council to "snitch" and the perception that they did "snitch" was an obstacle for council participation and support.

UNCLEAR RESPONSIBILITY: THE GRASS INCIDENT

Part of the misunderstanding of lack of leadership could be what I call the "grass incident." The grass incident exemplifies what happens when the housing authority officials and community workers are unclear about the responsibilities of the resident council regarding maintenance issues. My field notes from the April 23 council meeting record the following incident:

An issue that Linda brought up after the council meeting was the grass not being mowed. I'll admit, the high grass makes this place look worse; it's not very attractive at all. Personally, I can't understand why it isn't cut. At the meeting today, Linda discussed how snakes can and do hide out in the grass and that kids who have bad allergies, their allergies start to act up. For some reason, Rivertown was not getting the grass mowed by the maintenance staff, which is operated by the housing authority. Linda was getting upset that the grass wasn't being mowed and she didn't want her grandchildren playing out in the grass. Besides her personally wanting to do something about the grass situation, other residents in the community were coming to her complaining about the grass.

Being fed up with the grass not being mowed and concerned for her grandchildren's safety, Linda organized a petition demanding that the development's grass be mowed, and soon thereafter the task was undertaken. As Linda described the situation:

They [residents in Rivertown] knew that I could do something about it. But they didn't want to go to any meetings to say, well, you know, we need to do this. But when I took the paper around to get people to sign it, "Oh yeah, we'll sign it so this grass can be cut." They voluntarily signed the paper. They were willing to do that.

Sam suggested that the grass incident was a maintenance issue rather than one that should have been sent before the council. He indicated that

the resident council didn't have nothing to do with grass cutting. She [Linda] been saying for [a while that]—she wanted her grass cut because she was a resident. She just wanted her grass cut, period. Our job is to make sure that it's [resident council] for the kids and their families. Now the grass is a maintenance problem. Yeah, that's for management and them to work through with that when they stepped over bounds and they got in hot water and the issue got out of hand.

For Sam, then, the mowing of the grass was something for which the housing authority rather than the resident council should have been responsible. Unlike Sam, both Alvin and Maynard thought the grass incident was a resident council issue. According to Alvin:

And if the people in Rivertown at a certain point in time say, "We're not pleased with the way our grass is being cut or the way that it looks" that is a resident council issue because the resident council can work with the housing authority to say, "What is the policy? How often should the grass be cut? And come on over here and look at the grass. And are you saying that this is acceptable?"

In fact, Linda did call the housing authority and talk to the manager about the grass situation. When she did, however, the manager did not respond as though the issue was an important one, so Linda sought assistance elsewhere. She explained:

I'm not satisfied with the manager. I'll call up to the housing authority and explain what I'm in the process of doing. This is wrong. I think this is wrong. My manager says that it's not wrong. Or I want to speak to someone that is over her to see exactly where we stand on this.

The grass incident became a concern for Linda because of her young grandchildren, and in turn she brought it up in a council meeting as a result of the members' long-standing concern for children in the community. On the one hand, then, it seems the issue was one that could easily have been within the scope of the council's responsibilities. However, Sam did not perceive the issue in the same way, and his perception likewise had some grounding. All community maintenance issues were, in fact, tied to the funding and organizational structure of the housing authority. Discussing a grass incident that happened at another public housing community, Alvin said:

> What I had to do was let the folks know about the current changes that took place on the maintenance crew which changed from somebody being on the development and cutting their grass every week to a team being formed which travels federal around to each site. And we had to educate them on the reasons why the changes occurred, which basically dealt with federal money being taken away.

Maynard expressed his belief that the role of the resident council should be extended beyond the narrow definition assigned to it by its members. Discussing the role of the council and the grass incident, he said:

> The resident council should have been on it [grass situation] before the residents . . . issues like that, those are small issues. Issues of the grass not being cut, those are obvious things that the resident council should be on top of. But when a resident feels that their rights are being violated or the resident is having some personal issues. They just want to know what some resources are. . . . I need computer training. Where can I go to get computer training? Those are the type of issues that residents should be coming to the resident councils about. You know, the grass, everybody can see that. It's a shame that a resident even has to go to a council member in order for them to do something about it. They should have been doing something about that already.

For Maynard, two issues emerged from this incident: (1) resident council members should be in tune with everything that goes on in the community and (2) they should be empowering the residents on a larger, life-altering scale. Once again, however, one must remember that the council itself established that its mission was to help the children in the community. In addition, because the council was small, with rotating members, it did not have the resources or the time to concern itself with everything that occured at Rivertown. Perhaps if the council was bigger, the members could concern themselves with all facets of community life, but under the present circumstances that was impossible.

In Maynard's opinion, the primary role of the council should be to empower the community and, as a result, all its efforts should focus on developing empowerment strategies and promoting self-sufficiency regarding such issues as life skills, job skills, and resource development. Once again, however, the council's members did not see that as their role. Coming from New Orleans, Maynard had seen numerous examples of severely distressed public housing, characterized by the National Commission on Severely Distressed Public Housing (1992) as possessing violent crime and drug problems, high vacancy rates, physical deterioration, and high rates of unemployment and poverty. Rivertown does not fit the definition of severely distressed housing;

hence Maynard's expectations for what should be accomplished by the council members to empower their community was affected by his previous understanding and assumptions about public housing.

Empowerment can mean different things to different people. Foster-Fishman et al. (1998, 508) state that "empowerment assumes divergent forms and meanings across people, is contextually determined, and changes over time." Who ultimately was responsible for getting the grass mowed is unknown. However, Linda's concern for the safety of her grandchildren, consistent with the resident council's focus on children, demonstrated that she was empowered, not lazy or unmotivated, and her actions led to getting the grass cut.

The roles and responsibilities of the housing authority officials and resident council members must be more clearly defined. To begin with, housing authority officials must draft clearer guidelines delineating the parameters of their roles within the council and responsibilities to it. Likewise, council members must draft guidelines outlining their own roles and responsibilities. Such a process could be undertaken more effectively by an outside consultant with no ties to either group—someone who could objectively assess the two groups and offer guidelines based upon those interpretations.

Also, measures must be undertaken to dispel the conception that council members were "snitches" who reported directly to the housing authority. Care must be taken to articulate clearly and strongly to all residents an awareness of the fact that the council was a self-governing body whose sole responsibility was bettering the life of the community as a whole—not reporting lease violations, problems, or the sorts of activities best left to management. Only when all members of the community were made aware of this fact could trust build between all involved parties.

Critical race theory (CRT) admonishes us to look for how racialized assumptions associated with race, class, poverty, and public housing manifested themselves in Rivertown. Despite Maynard, Alvin, and Jane agreeing with the CFR, they held their own stereotypical assumptions about public housing and its residents. For example, Jane stereotyped and stigmatized the residents in public housing. As a resident council coordinator, her assumptions shaped how she interacted with the members of the resident council and the community in general. According to her, all such individuals were depressed and came from "bad situations." She said:

> Now from the housing authority's perspective you're dealing with people who, going back to depression again, depression makes you apathetic and indifferent, and you don't care. They're there because they don't care uh their self-esteem is low, their resources are low, there are many of the folks there that have gotten there because they've, they sold out a long time ago to a boyfriend, to a pimp, to a the school system you know they just said okay you know I'll do whatever you want me to do I can't make decisions for myself so

you tell me what to do. And, it's just you know they've gotten tossed aside and now they're here and the housing authority is saying here are the rules.

Since I did not interview all the residents of Rivertown, I can vouch only for the resident council members and some of the residents that I got to know: no one sold out to a boyfriend or pimp. Domestic violence and economic hard times were some of the reasons why the council members and some of the residents were forced to live in public housing. Additionally, Jane believed people are "depressed." Mental illness was a factor that led to staying in public housing, but in context, Jane's discussion of depression sounded more like she was referring to an attitude, not an illness. Even though she hinted at structural factors such as schools or other systems that have "tossed [them] aside," she arrived at the incorrect conclusion that it was absurd for the housing authority to let "these people" address community issues and give advice to the housing authority. Perhaps that was why Jane felt it was her responsibility to lead the council—she considered them incapable of thinking for themselves. Her internalization of stereotypes and stigmas regarding the poor shaped her assumptions about the residents of public housing, which affected her ability to act as a support mechanism for the council.

Maynard made the assumption that by focusing solely on children, the council was taking the easy way out because children are easier to control than adults. Instead of sharing their focus and helping them work toward improving the lives of the children, Maynard tried to push the council members toward his views. For him, the council should be "on top" of everything that went on in the community. Because the resident council, for a variety of reasons including not sharing this view, was not "on top" of everything, Maynard did not see it as effective. If he had shared the council's vision of what was best for the community, the council might have achieved more than it did. Rather than hearing the voices of the council members, Maynard focused on his own perceptions and assumptions regarding public housing and public housing residents that derived in large part from his experience with the severely distressed public housing communities of New Orleans.

Alvin also thought the purpose of the council should move beyond children. He thought the council should serve as a policing agent in the community and report lease violations and any crimes in the area. In spite of the relatively low rates of crime and violence in Rivertown, Alvin assumed, based on stereotypes and stigmas of public housing, that problems were so severe that they could get quickly out of hand if all agents of social control, including the resident council, were not constantly policing the community.

On the surface, the CFR shows no indication that it is anything but neutral, objective, and color blind. However, as critical race theory would suggest, the individuals tasked with implementing and enforcing the rules and regulations are not neutral, objective, or color blind. Although the housing officials seemed to be well-meaning, hardworking, and caring individuals, structural limitations and their own stereotypical assumptions of public housing residents led them to prioritizing their views over those of the council.

Although the housing officials may have been aware of many of the factors that led to the residents being in the community, this awareness was not utilized in their dealings with the resident council. Critical race theory suggests that when history and lived experiences of marginalized groups are ignored, then racialized interpretations of the law are more apt to occur. Housing officials were almost silent on expressing sympathetic understanding of the problems in the lives of the resident council members. Jane tried to show, with mixed success, that she understood how the residents came to be in Rivertown, but her analysis of their behavior once here was less than complimentary. The housing officials spoke of their own overwork; they did not speak of the hard work that the resident council members were doing given the difficult lives of the members themselves. They seemed not to be aware of the group's lived experiences. It is not surprising then, that they did not appreciate the resident council members' focus on children. Granted, sometimes the resident council received assistance and money from officials, but my analysis revealed no indication that efforts were made to find out why the council prioritized the children. Not understanding the council members' experiences further perpetuated false, stereotypical assumptions made by the housing authority officials and community workers. CRT allows us to see how embedded in such assumptions are racialized stereotypes and stigmas about the poor and people who live in public housing.

NOTES

1. Snitching will be discussed.
2. *Rucker v. Davis* 1998.
3. All these issues are discussed throughout this book.

Chapter Four

Rules for Organizing a Council

Besides laws and policies that define the role and responsibilities of the resident council and housing authority, there are also laws that define the legal purpose, structure, and importance of the resident council.

HUD and the Ridgeway Housing Authority recognize and support the resident council as a community liaison designed to improve the quality of life for residents of public housing and promote communities self-sufficiency initiatives from within. HUD legally recognizes the resident council as the sole representative of the public housing community. As a result of this privileged status, in order to support and strengthen council activities, HUD allocates federal monies to the housing authorities, which they budget each year to fund resident participation. Section 964.18 of the *Code of Federal Regulations* states:

964.18 HA role in activities under subparts B & C.

(a) HAs with 250 units or more.
(1) A HA shall officially recognize a duly elected resident council as the sole representative of the residents it purports to represent, and support its tenant participation activities.
(2) When requested by residents, a HA shall provide appropriate guidance to residents to assist them in establishing and maintaining a resident council. . . .
(7) In no event shall HUD or a HA recognize a competing resident council once a duly elected resident council has been established. Any funding of resident activities and resident input into decisions concerning public housing operations shall be made only through the officially recognized resident council. . . .

(b) HAs with fewer than 250 units.

(1) HAs with fewer than 250 units[1] of public housing have the option of participating in programs under this part.

(2) HAs shall not deny residents the opportunity to organize. If the residents decide to organize and form a resident council, the HA shall comply with the following:

(i) A HA shall officially recognize a duly elected resident council as the sole representative of the residents it purports to represent, and support its tenant participation activities.

(ii) When requested by residents, a HA shall provide appropriate guidance to residents to assist them in establishing and maintaining a resident council. (24 C.F.R. 964.18)

In order for a resident council to (a) be officially recognized and (b) be eligible to receive HUD funding, which is budgeted and distributed through the Ridgeway Housing Authority, it must meet two requirements: (1) the election of resident council members and (2) the creation of meeting obligations. Actually, those two elements are intertwined. There are specific rules and procedures for duly electing a resident council.

Once elected, in order to receive funding, each resident council must meet certain requirements set forth by its housing authority. Hence, the Ridgeway Housing Authority requires the following:

1. An annual budget approved and signed by the appropriate persons
2. An annual written agreement, approved and signed by the appropriate persons
3. That the council is composed of at least five and no more than eleven active members
4. That at least one representative from the council is present at the applicable joint resident council meetings
5. That at least one representative from the council is present at the applicable site-based planning meetings

BYLAWS, GREEN BOOK, AND MEETING
LEGAL UNDERSTANDING

Organizing and attending meetings were a major job requirement of the resident council. Meetings are stressed in the *Code of Federal Regulations*, bylaws, and the Green Book. The policies articulate how the resident council members should have control of the meetings, how they should meet regularly, and how they should involve the community. Nonetheless, the requirements and expectations of meetings and the reality of them were another area of disjunction. Numerous factors contributed to this disjunction.

Green Book and Bylaws

To help the resident councils conduct efficient and organized meetings, keep them informed about policies and laws that govern the council, and permit them to comply with HUD regulations, Jane helped create what is known as the "Green Book." The Green Book is highly stressed by the managers, community workers, and housing authority officials. When I first began this project, I had no idea what this book was—however, the way all housing officials referred to it, I began to believe it was not green but golden. For example, in describing the importance of the Green Book, Maynard said:

> Green book, it describes everything about a resident council. It tells them how to hold election, it gives them an outline of what their bylaws should include, it gives them scenarios on how to conduct meetings. And none of them had went through that [training on the Green book]. So they[2] were just winging their meetings. They would hold meetings and people would come out and not come back again because it was totally unorganized. So I've been conducting workshops, have been going through that Green Book with them, so that they can become more familiar. And if they can just get that then later on we could work on CFR 964-whatever later on down the line. But right now we just have to get them in the basic operations of a resident council.

In reality, the Green Book is a green two-inch binder that contains printed information, including rules and laws, regarding productive and efficient council meetings. The binder has ten colorful tabs that divide the organized sections of information. When you first open this double-pocket binder, you find information about the Ridgeway Housing Authority, including phone numbers and names of people who work at the housing authority, information on their mission, and a brief history and description of the housing authority and its upward mobility programs for residents. After you get through eleven pages of background information, you arrive at a table of contents, which offers a breakdown of the ten sections included therein:

1. Notes
2. Information about Your Neighborhood
3. Directory of Names and Addresses
4. Forms
5. Fliers, Announcements, Sign-In Sheets, etc.
6. Bylaws
7. Money Matters
8. Elections Process
9. Agreements and Other Documents
10. A Guide to a Strong Resident Council

In Section 10: A Guide to a Strong Resident Council, which was developed by the Pittsburgh field office, one finds bylaws, rules, and definitions of roles that can be held within the resident council. This section states, "It's important to note that a resident council should be run by the residents. The housing authority can only assist the council." In essence, everyone in the community should "assist" the council, but its members should run and organize it. Since resident councils are a self-sufficient organization, everyone involved with the council is a "supporting character." In other words, the council members themselves are responsible for organizing and determining the focus of the council.

Of course, the council can request the services of the manager and community workers. Managers can support the council with in-kind services, such as providing space, photocopying, and funding. According to the Green Book, the housing authority should respond promptly to reasonable requests, consult with council leaders on mutual problems, solicit suggestions from residents, and maintain channels of communication by meeting and discussing issues regularly. The rules for conducting meetings, receiving funding, and having a duly elected resident council are provided for in the Bylaws and Election Process.

Bylaws for the Meetings and Resident Council

The bylaws of the Rivertown Resident Council are composed of nine articles:

Article I: Name and Address
Article II: Purpose
Article III: Elections
Article IV: Interim Representatives and Officers
Article V: Obligations and Responsibilities
Article VI: Funding
Article VII: Meetings
Article VIII: Decisions
Article IX: Recall Procedures

The resident council members have to adhere to the bylaws, which lay the foundation for proper meeting procedures and for the election structure of the council. In defining the purpose of the bylaws, Sharon said:

> Each council has their own bylaws that they can make up. You know they're not a set of bylaws that are given to them by the Ridgeway Housing Authority. They make their own laws up so each community has a different set of laws.

Understanding Bylaws

Council members were given a draft of "HUD's Model Bylaws" so they could customize them to fit the needs of Rivertown; however, as of the date of this writing, the original model has not been altered. Council members simply adopted the bylaws that were given to them. The council members understood that bylaws are important, but not all of them understood why they are significant—and some of them simply did not understand them at all. For example, Sam thought the bylaws were useful, rather like the Bible. He thought that people were scared of them. He said:

> We got bylaws. I can look at the bylaws and tell you a whole lot 'cause see that's the thing, I think a whole lot of people don't want to get involved in it 'cause when you say bylaws you see what I'm saying when bylaws they think you talking about the law. See it's just like that for instance if I tell them to read the Bible see the Bible got laws in there and everything like that you shouldn't do.

At the same time Sam was aware of the need to understand the bylaws because, as he stated, "It's a whole lot and they said it changes all the time." He added:

> They got to read the bylaws and understand what they reading see. Now I can read a whole lot of stuff to somebody until they understand what it's saying it'd be like I can talk to that wall right there I'm not going to get no response. Maynard's got to come in here and explain it to, what things are about.

When I asked Jessica what would have helped her with the council, she told me that she "wanted someone to go over the bylaws" with her. She said, "Yeah, go over the bylaws. Yeah, it was useful, but some of it went right over my head . . . the bylaws and stuff." When I asked her if she knew what constitutes an official resident council she said, "No, not really. I know you're supposed to have stuff." Even though Linda explained certain elements of the official documents to Jessica, she said it still went over her head.

So it appears clear that while council members realized the importance of HUD bylaws to the governance structure of the meetings and to council activities, they did not always understand the laws themselves—a situation that could have contributed to council ineffectiveness. It was the duty of the HA officials to clarify and help them with bylaws and other forms of governance.

HUD RESPONSIBILITIES AND DUTIES

As a whole, members of the council did not believe or feel that the housing officials, community workers, and managers were performing their jobs. They reported receiving little to no help from these individuals. Sam talked about how the community workers, especially Maynard, never attended meetings. He also reported having some difficulty reaching Maynard:

> Well, see, when you, when you, ah, sent out a message for him, he [Maynard] didn't respond. And we, ah, e-mailed him and he didn't respond. And so you know and when we come to the meetings they say they comin' and they never showed up.

Sam understood that both Alvin and Maynard were supposed to help the council become more self-sufficient, but he asserted his belief that they did not do what they were paid to do. To this effect, he made an insightful comment: "I understand what he's [Maynard] saying about rely on him less but Maynard and Alvin they are getting paid to show us how to get the resident council up and going."

When I asked Linda to define Maynard's role and his responsibility to the council, she confessed that she had no idea what he did:

> I never could figure out what Maynard did. He never did anything for us. He'd call and make appointments and the only time he would keep 'em is if it was something he wanted. If he needed something. Like, when he needed something that I had, a paper he wanted, he would keep the appointment. If it was something that I needed he just didn't call me back at all. If he did call me, he wouldn't keep the appointment. The other lady that was, what was her name, she . . . we has a little thing going up here.

Whenever there was an "incident" involving neighbors in Rivertown, Linda knew that it was "the other lady's" (Sharon's) job to help resolve the conflict, but she wasn't sure what such a job truly entailed:

> It was their job to step in and try to resolve things with the families that were living here. I never did figure out what that was supposed to be [Sharon's role] because, well, Jessica had a slumber party down at the center one night, and I think Sharon came down for a little bit to that. She helped her set up, or something. . . . And I know they [Maynard and Sharon] go to Melrose Meetings.[3]

Jessica also concurred with her fellow council members that Maynard and Sharon were not particularly helpful to the group or to its efforts. When I asked Jessica to explain what these individuals might have done for the council and whether they had, in fact, helped the group's efforts, she replied:

Sharon more so than Maynard because, like you know, I asked her to come to the sleepover and do something. She's really good with that. Other than that, that's all that I've really talked to her about. She was willing to help me with the cooking classes and stuff like that, which that would have been good, but like I said, I got off the council before that happened.

Discussing Maynard, Jessica added that she would appreciate someone who would be more personal with the council. "He was just, I only really talked to him one time, and that was about goin' to the meetings," she said. "And he said either he or Sharon could come and get me or find somebody to take me." Although Maynard and Alvin were deemed ineffective by many members of the council, Sam expressed his opinion that these two individuals held the key to the empowerment of the council and to the community as a whole. In Sam's words, "Them the two keys, right there. Them the two links supposed to hook it up."

What exactly were the two supposed to "hook up"? In Sam's estimation, Maynard and Alvin were the avenues by which the council could gather the resources in order to accomplish its goal of helping the community's children. Before Jane left the housing authority, Sam and Linda had most of their interactions through her (Jessica joined the council after Jane left). Sam and Linda had constant issues with Jane, which later developed into an appreciation toward her. Sam said, "Everybody had issues with Jane. There this thing with me and Jane just like that there. See I always tell her like you know I just tell her straight up you know you want me to tell you how I feel about it? She said go ahead. I said well I'm gonna hurt your feelings. She said so, go ahead and hurt my feelings then. I just tell her you can't come in here and do what you wanna do." Linda said she did not like Jane at first because she "would give [me] attitude at first. But she helped me with the budget."

Of all the resident council meetings I attended, I remember seeing Jane at nearly every one. I recall seeing Sharon, Maynard, or Alvin only once[4]—this despite the fact that I was told on numerous occasions by Linda and Alvin that Maynard or Sharon was scheduled to attend. The lack of a "strong partnership" between the council and its "outside" cohorts, the community workers and housing officials, clearly is not in keeping with CFR 964.14 HUD Policy on Partnerships or with the mission or operation statement of Ridgeway. Regardless of the fact, however, that some council members believed that the housing authorities were less than diligent about their responsibilities, they did manage to plan several activities that focused on the community's children.

How can the council members organize and engage Rivertown residents in community activities when the job responsibilities of the housing authorities' officials are not being implemented?

Responsibilities and Structure

The job responsibilities of the housing authority officials, community workers, and managers are entwined with the structural dynamics of HUD, such
as federal funding, restructuring of the agency (HUD and Ridgeway Housing
Authority), and laws and policies that have to be enforced and implemented.
For example, because of limited resources, both Maynard and Alvin were
responsible for all the resident councils in all the public housing communities
in the city. Thus, due to the demands placed upon them, it became structurally impossible for them to achieve their job responsibilities.

The council members want someone to come to the meetings, help them
get organized, and explain all the laws and bylaws that they need to know.
The resident council members felt that the housing officials were not fulfilling this responsibility. When I asked Alvin and Maynard about their lack of
interaction with the council, they identified several reasons why they were
not always around, and they also shared their opinion as to why council
members would perceive them as being ineffective. Alvin and Maynard both
said that one of the reasons they had not been to Rivertown Council meetings
or more involved with the resident council was due to the organizational
structure and responsibilities of their positions: they must attend meetings
and work with over ten different public housing communities and resident
councils. Needless to say, they were extremely busy and were pulled in
multiple directions. Alvin acknowledged the difficulty of attending every
meeting:

> That is one of the most difficult things that I have to deal with and that is we
> have over ten communities and on a monthly basis if we had a resident council
> at all ten that would be 27 different meetings. A resident meeting, a resident
> council meeting, and a site-based meeting. It's impossible for me, right now,
> just with the councils that are active for me to attend every meeting because
> many are held at the same time, some are held when I'm at another meeting.

Maynard expressed his frustration: he realized he is just one person and
that he often could be difficult to reach:

> I mean, I'm dealing with over ten neighborhoods. So I am a very hard person
> to get ahold of. I can't guarantee that every time you want me to come that I'm
> going to be able to come. If my schedule is already . . . I mean, you know, just
> trying to do this interview you know how hard I am to get hold of. So . . . I am
> very busy and I am a very hard person to get ahold of, but if there's an issue
> that needs to be resolved, you know, one of the other communities, Anderson
> Hills, I did a workshop they weren't able to attend. They called me back and I
> rescheduled that particular workshop just for them. The workshop was for all
> of the communities. They couldn't make it, so they had some legitimate rea-
> sons. I rescheduled it. And I'm going back into their community and I'm going

to hold it for them. So I may not be able to do it when you want me to do it, but I am available to do it for you.

Maynard's role was to empower the resident council members by making them aware of their rights, the *Code of Federal Regulations*, and any other laws and policies that govern the resident council and public housing. However, because Maynard did not regularly attend meetings or return phone calls (for reasons explained above), the council members did not see him as effective. As a result, he was not able to carry out his role or fulfill his responsibility to them. Therefore, the council did not know its rights or fully understand the laws and policies that govern the council and the community. The resident council members interpreted Maynard's perceived lack of action to indicate that he did not care for or respect the council members. On the other hand, Maynard thought the resident council members themselves were responsible for empowering the community. In his opinion, they should have taken action and not been "lazy."

Alvin stated that he was hindered from doing his job for three reasons: (1) resident council members generally do not have telephones, (2) the past "history" between the council and the former resident coordinator had tainted the relationship, and (3) three people now did the job of the resident coordinator. According to Alvin:

> I'm hindered for a couple of different reasons. Number one, many of our resident council members do not have telephones. So if I have a conflict in just being able to call someone to say I won't be at the meeting, sometimes I can't. Sometimes I'll call the property manager to get a message, but then again the property manager isn't just sitting there waiting for me to take a message to someone else. So we find a lot of barriers that are there.

This may have been a problem with past resident councils, but the current council members of Rivertown all have telephones. They may not have an answering machine or message service, but they do have phones. A second barrier, according to Alvin, involved dealing with the history of the past community coordinator, Jane. Alvin elaborated:

> And we're also dealing with what happened in the past before I came on board and before Maynard and Sharon came on board. Jane Adams was the previous coordinator and she pretty much juggled the whole thing by herself. And I look back on that experience for Jane and I wonder how she was able to do what she did. Maynard and I meet every Friday at two o'clock here and we talk about what happened that week. Then we look at our calendars for the following week so we can just get adjusted. And that's been challenging for Maynard and I to go to as many meetings as we can along with the other job duties that we have. So we're juggling that day by day. And it's really hard to win over some of our residents because once they have just one negative experience, it's

hard to win their trust back. It's very hard. And for some they say, "I'm sorry but you blew it." And sometimes they'll tell you that and in other ways their body language will tell you that.

In the opinions of many resident council members, Jane was a one-woman army, and while it is true that now three people perform the job that she once did by herself, Maynard expressed the belief that she hindered the councils from being self-sufficient because she did everything for them. Discussing Jane, Maynard said:

> The council members that are on that council, the person that was before me, you know, in many ways she hindered a lot of the councils in that things that the council should have been doing to be more self-sufficient, she was doing for them. If they wanted to do a program, she would go out and make the program happen and say that the resident council did it.

For three years, the resident council members had a chance to become used to and comfortable with Jane's strong "hands-on" approach. As a result, when Maynard took his position, he faced some difficulty because his primary goal was to make the council more self-sufficient, a position directly opposite to the direction in which Jane took the group by, in his terms, "enabling" them:

> I don't work that way. If they want to do something, then I will give them the contact information, I will let them know who to contact, who to call to make it happen. If they need my help somewhere along the way of doing that, then I will be there for them. But they will never learn how to hold an election for their resident council, they'll never learn how to get a neighborhood watch started, if they don't do that themselves.

The third hindrance identified by Alvin involved how residents perceived the council, as well as previous negative experiences:

> Before I took this job I was a case manager here at Rivertown and we tried to partner up with the housing authority to help promote the resident council. And we used to go knocking on doors at least once a month. And many people would look at us and say, "Don't even mention the resident council." And some would explain and some wouldn't. Some would go into "I took an issue to them before and they never helped me" or "They snitched on me" or all kinds of stories. And what do you do when someone says that to you? It's hard to say, "Well, come on back and give 'em another try." They would say, "No, that's okay."

ROLE STRAIN: HOUSING AUTHORITY, COMMUNITY WORKERS, AND MANAGERS

Another area of disjunction involves the roles and responsibilities of the housing authority officials, community workers, and managers to the council. A role is an expected pattern or set of behaviors associated with a particular position or status (Major 2003). When multiple demands are placed on individuals, and they have "difficulty in fulfilling role obligations" (Goode 1960, 483) or they are forced by circumstance to adopt multiple roles, the result is *role strain*. Role strain is made up of *role overload* and *role conflict* (Sieber 1974). Researchers have devoted consideration attention to role strain, particularly that which is involved in the relationship between household division of labor and marital satisfaction (Stohs 2000; Piña and Bengtson 1993), religion (Edwards 2014), mental health and race (Copeland and Snyder 2011), and caregiving (Rozario, Morrow-Howell, and Hinterlong 2004). Since there are multiple demands and responsibilities placed on the HUD officials, role strain can affect their interactions with the council and interpretations of housing laws and policies.

Among the examples of "role strain" experienced by members of the housing authority, community workers, and managers were (1) abiding by the CFR and not having the manpower, financial support, or time to carry out the laws and policies, (2) taking on more responsibilities to help the residents and resident council members, and (3) conflicting views between personal assumptions and beliefs of the resident council and structural organization and policies of HUD/HAs. The multiple roles that the housing authority, community workers, and managers undertook came from structural changes imposed by the housing authority and HUD,[5] that affected their job responsibilities to the resident council. The role strain of job responsibilities led to several areas of disjunction, including not meeting responsibilities, unclear responsibilities, and blurred responsibilities.

Another area of disjunction involved policies and resources. Since there was a lack of funding and manpower, some of the housing officials and community workers were so overworked they could not meet their job responsibilities. Because they were overworked, they could not come to meetings and help the resident council. As Maynard demonstrated, his job responsibility was to assist the council so they could empower the residents in the community. He was supposed to "translate" all the laws and policies for the council, so that the council could know what was expected and how to do what was expected, and pass information to the residents as needed. Since he was one person working in several communities, he had difficulty attending meetings. As a result of Maynard being unable to perform his job successfully, the council was unable to receive the information it needed in a timely and efficient manner.

FUNDING AND THE RESIDENT COUNCIL

To support and encourage resident councils to build communities, HUD has provided funding and offered numerous programs and opportunities. Some of the housing authority officials, managers, and community workers thought that Rivertown Resident Council members were not talking full advantage of their opportunities, while others thought the laws and policies themselves were problematic. LaTonya suggested that residents were not taking advantage of the funds that were already available. She said:

> We have funds there for the resident council so we can do things in the community for the residents and if we don't have a council or body then the residents won't get those funds to do the extracurricular activities that we do.

LaTonya thought the housing authority was doing an exceptional job of providing funding to the resident councils. Furthermore, she believed that lack of community support hindered residents from taking full advantage of the funding opportunities. In her opinion:

> I think the housing authority is really great as far as trying to back up the council in the community, trying to give them what they need to get operating and going. But, the problem is the lack of support that we get from our, I guess, the residents within the community to participate. I mean it's there for us. Like, you know, the resident council body's there, the funds are there for them to utilize for the community, but you just got to get the people to want to participate and take advantage of that so I think the housing authority is doing a great job as far as making it available to them. But, as far as them acting it out and carrying it out that's where we are lacking.

In comparison, Vanessa thought that funding did not matter if the council members and residents did not buy into the purpose/role of the council. She said:

> The residents have to buy into this. They're not doing it because HUD says it's so important for the housing authority to have these resident councils and all this money in the resident council. The resident council at Rivertown, they really didn't focus that much on the criteria that HUD put out there. They just did it because they wanted to make a difference and they had a little extra time that they could give. And that's where it stopped. There's a whole lot of rhetoric and if you're poor and you're living in public housing and you're on the resident council, so what if they've got all this money and all these guidelines and all this stuff that the housing authority needs to have done.

One incentive for joining the council and helping the community is money: council members do receive a small stipend for serving and they receive money for planning various activities and programs to help their communities. Regardless of the fact that it helps some, money alone is not an incentive to get residents to join the council. If money was indeed a deciding factor, then one could expect residents in the community to fight for a place on the council. In actuality, however, in recompense for its time and efforts, the council receives only $100 a month,[6] which active members then have to split among themselves. Members do admit, though, that even this small amount proves vital at times. "It was $100 a month and we divided it evenly among all of us," Linda said. "Yeah. It helped. Well, it helped [the stipend money she got from the council]. I did rent credit and got most of my rent paid by getting rent credit. And then I got, what was it, $30 or something."

When it comes to dividing the money, council members do not quibble over amounts. Linda told me about how members strove to divide the money evenly:

> All the time that I was on the council we agreed at the beginning that . . . they said we could let Sam do something, we could give him $50 and split the rest of the money. Like if I did something, I could take the whole $100 for that month and vice versa. But we didn't want to do that because it was, we didn't want to have a conflict with each other about "I did more than you" and stuff like that. It was easier to split even if somebody didn't do anything, we still went ahead and split the money with them because that was what we agreed on to keep from having conflict with money.

In addition to receiving this small monetary compensation, council members can apply for grants or are automatically eligible for public funding of self-improvement projects. However, Vanessa commented that the council often overlooked or ignored opportunities that would help them advance individually and permit them to better assist residents. For example, she recalled how the council did not take advantage of available monies with which they could purchase a computer and obtain computer training. She indicated that Linda was the only person to use the money for computer training. For various reasons—work, transportation issues, child-care responsibilities, scheduling—Sam and Jessica were never able to undertake the training. Linda was placed in charge of buying the computer and getting things organized, then each of the council members received $200 worth of training. Although Linda did participate in training, her experience suggested that she received few benefits from it:

> We had money left over from our computer training. I went ahead and took my $200 computer training and I forgot everything. I don't even know how to get back in. I forget. . . . I learned how to load a disk and get it off on it and save it.
>
> Nobody else took their training. We had $1,000 for council training. And nobody else took their training. I went ahead and bought a new computer with the money that was to buy the computer and then I bought a disk and another

book. It's still here. Nobody's asked for it, so I haven't taken it down there [resident council office].

The failure of some council members to undertake free computer training suggests that members often have goals far different from those expected of them by community workers and housing authority officials, who see them as the mechanism by which improvement can be brought to all community members. While housing authority officials and community workers sometimes see the council as less than effective, members of the latter group often view those from the former two groups in the same light. Clearly, the groups have different perspectives on a variety of issues. The next chapter will compare areas of disjunction between the groups that may act as obstacles that prevent council members from fulfilling HUD's expectations for them as community builders.

NOTES

1. Section 964.18 b and 2(i)(ii) state the same thing for HAs with fewer than 250 units.

2. Maynard was discussing a meeting he went to at Summit Hills, one of the public housing communities. The resident council was not trained on the Green Book.

3. The Melrose Meeting is where the council members had to go for the joint resident council meetings. Meetings are discussed in chapter 6.

4. This was at a site-based meeting, not regular council meeting. Going through my field notes, I found that Maynard and Sharon never showed up at the meetings. If they did attend, I was not present at the regular meetings.

5. Since the housing authorities receive federal monies, changes in federal laws and policies have an effect on the manpower and monies that the Ridgeway Housing Authority receives.

6. The councils are also allocated funds for community-building activities, which is separate from the money they get when they volunteer.

Chapter Five

Not Fitting the Public Housing Image: Location and Communication

The lack of attention and funding Rivertown receives from the housing authority is another source of disjunction between expectations and realities. I posit that the reason for this lack of attention, relative to some other public housing communities in Ridgeway, derives in part from the location of Rivertown but also from its failure to receive a HOPE VI grant.

LOCATING RIVERTOWN

As noted previously, Rivertown is situated far away from other public housing communities and downtown Ridgeway. The location can be described as both "suburban" and "semirural"; in fact, Rivertown is a hop, skip, and a jump from the Ridgeway County line. In other words, Rivertown is on the edge of the city limits. Alvin, Vanessa, and Jane all commented on how the physical location of Rivertown impacted the effectiveness of information distribution to the resident council. Alvin suggested that the physical distance of Rivertown caused its residents to draw less attention and resources than those in the other, more urban public housing communities. Because Rivertown is the farthest away, it is out of sight, out of mind. In Alvin's terms:

> I think it's, for some, it's almost the out of sight out of mind where to get to Rivertown you've got to have a reason for going there, where some of our communities we might pass them going somewhere else. Like Winton Park. We have probably eight or nine employees here that mentor some of the kids at Winton Park Elementary School, where every week when we go we pass that development. So if there's something going on in that development let's say appearance-wise, that's a concern. We see it, we come back to the office,

we mention it to somebody, and the wheels start turning. Where Rivertown is located, West Chester is close, but you pass West Chester before you get to Rivertown so you don't have the same kind of interaction. The only time I myself go to Rivertown is when I'm meeting with a resident or I have a purpose for going out there. But I pass West Chester almost every day when I go to work. I pass Forest Park on the interstate. I pass Oakland[1] on the interstate. So a lot of times it's just the recognition of something is going on, something is out of sync, or something doesn't look right. A lot of times that leads to other conversations.

Location and environment can affect many facets of a person's life. For example, Grice and Skinner (1998) note that the environment can detract from effective communication. Alvin's statement suggests that this was true for the Rivertown Resident Council. Vanessa commented on how Rivertown was in its own little cul-de-sac. "Down here we are [isolated], but each housing development is like that, except for the high rises," she said. "We're in our own little world."

Vanessa also realized that if Rivertown was located closer to a big city or a more progressive area, the information shared by and interaction of the managers with the resident council and the community would be a lot different. Vanessa believed much to be affected by a combination of both location and the mind-set of the people with whom she worked. In her estimation:

I think because of the location of where we are, I think that if we were in Northern City, I think it would be totally different. I know it would be totally different. Still the location of where we are and the mind-set of your supervisor plays a big role on how respectful the staff will be. That's key right there. If you've got a jerk or someone who is narrow minded for your supervisor, you can't expect to grow. But that's something that I found that I had to tolerate.

Unlike Alvin and Vanessa, Jane believed Rivertown to be in a good location as far as conveniences offered the community. She saw the location of Rivertown as better than that of some of the other communities because it provides residents with conveniences unique to place:

There are physical things too like they're right next to a grocery store. Just up the street from the laundry mat as opposed to the folks at West Chester with no grocery store anywhere near them, no laundry mat anywhere near them. People who have no car are really stuck. You have to carry your laundry on the bus, you have to carry your groceries on the bus and it gets old.

Jane also believed, however, that with regard to location, the council and the residents they served might also receive less attention from the "outside," including assistive agencies, because unlike other communities in the area, Rivertown is not located in a chaotic environment that draws the attention (both good and bad). Additionally, Jane suggested that this lack of chaos—while very good in the larger sense—might also lead to complacency on the part of residents and council members. In her opinion:

> It wasn't chaotic um if anything it was just the opposite. Um it wasn't chaotic enough. Um they were—everybody was too compliant too um and I don't know as they say the physical makeup of the community um they didn't have to deal with some of the issues that, that other neighborhoods had to deal with so there was a level of I guess stability. It's just not an area of expertise for me, but it would stand to reason the quality of life would be different in a community where your basic needs for food and laundry and transportation there's a river over there um there are things at Rivertown . . . and that beautiful playing field—the dynamics of that community are gonna be very different than the dynamics at Winton Park. There's no open area where kids can play, where there's a heavily traffic street cutting right through the neighborhood, no grocery store, no laundry mat, no um so different kind of person is gonna want to live there for starters um and maybe be more content living there and feel less.

Distance, location, and visibility (or lack thereof) might help describe why Rivertown and its council members may not receive a lot of attention from the housing authority. On top of that, Rivertown is not known for possessing an attention-getting, chaotic environment. Issues of drugs and crime are major concerns for severely distressed housing, but they do not seem to affect the residents of Rivertown. Severely distressed public housing is characterized by the National Commission on Severely Distressed Public Housing (1992) as possessing violent crime and drug problems, high vacancy rates, physical deterioration, and high rates of unemployment and poverty. Although some of these features might describe Rivertown—unemployment, some physical deterioration of the site—clearly others do not. The location of Rivertown was directly connected to the attention or lack thereof that its residents and council members receive, whether monetary or programmatic. Its semirural location, away from more urban housing developments, and its reputation as a relatively peaceful community also—quite ironically—have made Rivertown (and thus its needs) less visible to housing officials. In an odd sense, Rivertown has been penalized monetarily and programmatically for not being a stereotypical public housing community.

In addition to these factors, Rivertown council members faced another problem: how to make the council known to residents.

HOPE VI GRANT

In 1992 the National Commission on Severely Distressed Housing submitted a report to Congress that determined that "6 percent of the 1.4 million existing public housing dwellings (about 86,000 units) were in severely distressed conditions." To assist in these communities, the commission recommended the removing and replacing of such units; the revitalization of the community in three general areas (physical improvements, management improvements, and social and community services to address residents' needs); and funding of over five billion dollars, carried out over a ten-year period (HUD 2003a).

As a result of the report, in 1993 the Urban Revitalization Demonstration Program (URD)—which is also known as the HOPE VI Program—was created by the Departments of Veterans Affairs, Housing and Urban Development (HUD), and the Independent Agencies Appropriations Act (Pub. L. No. 102-389). Under this act, housing authorities can apply for two types of grants: HOPE VI revitalization grant and HOPE VI demolition grant. The revitalization grant funds the "capital cost of major rehabilitation, new construction, and other physical improvements, the demolition of severely distressed public housing, management improvements; planning and technical assistance, and community supportive services with the skills and support they need to become self-sufficient." The HOPE VI demolition grant provides funds to demolish obsolete public housing units.

When the Quality Housing and Work Responsibility Act (QHWRA)[2] was passed in 1998, funding requirements were amended to include this act. Through the QHWRA, public housing communities that receive HOPE VI grants also have to prove that support and social services exist that can help residents make the transition from welfare to work and become self-sufficient. After receiving this grant, the community goes through both physical and social changes.

In March 1998, HUD received 101 applications from severely distressed public housing communities requesting $1.9 billion in assistance. Only twenty HOPE VI revitalization grants were given that year, which totaled over $507 million (HUD 2003a). One of the twenty housing authorities to receive grant funding that year was the Ridgeway Housing Authority, which received over $15 million to renovate Quebec Gardens. The total cost of revitalization of Quebec Gardens was $45 million, with the remaining $30 million above and beyond the Hope VI grant to come from the city, county, and private donors.

With the grant, the Ridgeway Housing Authority was able to "demolish 126 units and [replace] them with 34 lease/purchase units for public housing residents (24 on site and 10 off site), 24 market rental units, and 44 market rate homeownership units off-site. The remaining 174 public housing units will undergo extensive rehabilitation. In conjunction with the HOPE VI activities the housing authority established a one-stop-shop Opportunity Center to further revitalize the surrounding community" (HUD 2003a).

Receiving this grant meant tremendous media attention, and also that a lot of involvement from the city of Ridgeway, the resident council, and the residents of Quebec Gardens, was necessary for all the changes that were to occur in the community—and it definitely occurred. One of the reasons that the grant prompted additional involvement is that embedded in the rules for receiving it is a requirement for active involvement of the resident councils.[3]

Besides looking better structurally, Quebec Gardens now has an on-site day-care facility, provides job training, and offers other services for people who live in the new community—all features of the HOPE VI requirements.

Needless to say, Quebec Gardens received a lot of attention, invested monies, and benefits. Sharon commented on this:

> Quebec Gardens [is] where they have the self-sufficiency program where people um once you join this program you have to work you have to get a job you know and it helps you ah you can stay in the community for like five years and they give you assistance with child care and different things like that. So, you have a group of people living in this community that's more progressive in their lives and the community looks like it too. You see the community there's no trash and it looks nice. They already put a ton of money in it to refurbish it, to make it look nice they're keeping it up though. They're keeping it looking nice it's not going back down so I think because of the program that's put in place, it makes the people think more progressively and their community reflects that.

Sharon also admitted that maybe in the next year or so attention could be focused on Rivertown. She said:

> I just think their community has lots of potential and ah maybe within the next year sometime um we're gonna try and focus on Rivertown and hopefully we can search the community and find it's a potential. You find people who are willing to help it to get to its potential—its fullest potential and make it a better community. But, I think it could be really great over there.

Daniel said that he would like the other public housing communities to be a part of the self-sufficiency program now in operation at Quebec 2000. He realized that monies and resources would make a big difference. He noted:

> Oh, it would be nice if they could be. It would be nice. It would take a lot more staff to try to push a program like that. You know, most housing authorities, right now, because of budget cuts and things, most housing authorities have on staff property managers. People can manage the development. But as far as doing other programs, you have to kind of depend on other agencies you can refer people to. But in Quebec, we have staff over at Quebec that specifically work with self-sufficiency. Which makes a difference.

As of now, however, the housing authority cannot afford the monies or resources that would be required to help Rivertown.

Resident council members Jessica and Sam expressed their beliefs that in the wake of the grant, Quebec Gardens received all of the housing authority's

benefits and attention, while Rivertown continued to receive little of either. For example, Jessica said she wished her community at least offered child-care services for working mothers. "I'd like to see Rivertown have like a little child-care center and, like, that's over there in Quebec Gardens. That'd be great. This community is so big, I don't see why they don't have one." Likewise, Sam expressed the pangs of feeling personally ignored: "Well see I guess when they started on Quebec 2000 everybody went to Quebec 2000 they forgot about Rivertown they forgot about Winton Hills they forgot about West Chester, forgot about all the other developments." He added: "See and now and the thing about that I was telling the manager over here we need some of the same things that Quebec 2000 has."

There are numerous laws, policies, programs, and grants to help resident council members and residents of public housing improve their living environment and assist individuals and families in achieving economic self-sufficiency. One such grant is HOPE VI. Since one of the other local public housing communities, Quebec Gardens, received this prestigious grant, Rivertown did not receive much attention or funding in comparison. Because the housing authority was focused on implementing the HOPE VI grant, the focus on Rivertown changed. Since Rivertown is located away from other public housing communities rather than in a "stereotypical" chaotic public housing neighborhood, it does not have the reputation of being an eyesore, nor is it thought of as a "pain" by housing authority officials. However, these positive assessments have done little to help residents and serve, in fact, as a double-edged sword in the game of funding and assistance. Ironically, perhaps due in great part to its positive attributes, Rivertown has been largely overlooked by officials, who have been focused on renovating severely distressed local housing. Extant public housing policies have not provided Rivertown with the support of other public housing communities, such as receiving a Hope VI grant. Given that such an influx of funds and attention can be energizing for resident councils, then conversely, the lack of these may have contributed to the inertia demonstrated at times by the Rivertown Resident Council.

COMMUNICATION DISCONNECTION

Broken Communication Bridge

Another area of disjunction with respect to residents becoming involved with the resident council deals with how information about the council meetings is communicated and advertised to the community. Having regular and open lines of shared communication and information is essential for the empowerment and self-sufficiency of the resident council and the public housing community as a whole.

It is the responsibility of such individuals as Maynard, Alvin, Jane, and the managers to keep such lines to the council open and unimpeded by bureaucratic "red tape." Information has to be understood and communicated not only to the council members themselves but also to the residents of Rivertown, managers, housing authority officials, and community workers. In other words, all channels of communication—both to and from—must remain open.

Whether intentional or not, a communication break existed between the Rivertown Resident Council and housing authority officials, managers, community workers, and the residents of Rivertown. This proved extremely problematic, because HUD and the housing authority stress self-sufficiency and the empowerment of the resident council, which depends on a strong line of communication.

Given that the managers, housing authority officials, and community workers often hold predetermined assumptions regarding residents of their communities and that they often communicate in large part based upon those assumptions, they might or might not be effective communicators. For instance, when Vanessa left, some of the council members did not know she had gone, and the residents in general had no idea about the change in management. When LaTonya came in, she sent out letters to inform the community that she was the new manager. Then without notice, LaTonya left, and Dixie came in. Although LaTonya made an attempt to announce her assumption of the position of manager, by and large, such changes in management are not communicated to the residents as they should be.

Of course, not all communication should occur between "officials" and resident council members alone. An essential component of the communication structure that governs any housing complex should be the one between resident council members and the residents themselves. Councils members, HUD, and the HA want residents to participate at meetings and in their community, voice their concerns, and be informed about issues that affect them. At Rivertown, although attempts were made to encourage participation by residents—for example, council members would routinely send out flyers about meetings and events in the community—the majority of the adult residents did not attend meetings or participate in community events.[4] The council members even tried such "gimmicks" as having free food and prizes to entice the adult residents to come to meetings, but nothing seemed to work. In fact, in the over two years I studied Rivertown, I can count on one hand the number of times residents attended meetings at which I was present. Although the resident council had attempted to announce events via flyers, the structure of the meetings themselves and the relationship between the council and the manager also contributed to the miscommunication that prevailed in the relationship between council members and residents. Yet council members persisted in their attempts to communicate.

Communication: Advertising the Council

In order to create a successful resident council, those involved must ensure that residents fully understand the purpose, role, and responsibilities of the council. Despite everything the council did to distribute information about meetings and community-wide events, residents in the community did not attend Rivertown Council meetings or participate in community activities. Sharon said she believed that residents didn't come to the meetings because they didn't see any actions from the council and they didn't know what was going on. "I think some of them do, but the ones that do I don't think they really care," she said. "I don't know if they know the effectiveness of a resident council in their community and the benefit of having a resident council, so they really don't care 'cause they don't see anything happening, you know."

LaTonya realized that perhaps management might be contributing to the inconsistency of the resident council. Even Daniel agreed that a better method for communication between residents and council members must be discovered. He stressed that HUD needed to create specific policies regarding communicating or suggest a process by which councils could more effectively recruit people. He said:

> In my opinion, and you know, HUD needs to come out with a way to select resident council members. In other words, not so much as who to vote on and stuff like that. How do you recruit me as a resident council? What do you look at in a resident council member? "Okay, you're going to be on the resident council. I don't have but three people and need six." I think it's a bit more than communication. I think that even with the communication, if you don't have a way of selecting the people, you still not going to get anywhere. In other words, you can put out all kinds of flyers. We have done things like take kids out to the play they had last year. We sent flyers out to everybody in the development. I bet we didn't get 50 kids, all told. And we was going to provide transportation and get them there. It's the Jackie Robinson story. We wound up getting kids like from the schools and other locations to go because we wanted to fill the house up. But a lot of them were not the kids from our developments.

KNOCKING ON DOORS

In the absence of a more effective mechanism, one quick way to communicate information to residents is through flyers, although the method has its drawbacks. Information is always posted in the community room about events but unless a resident actually visits the site on a regular basis, this line of communication breaks down. Regardless, since some residents work irregular hours or they may not have phones, passing out flyers and knocking on doors still proved the best communicative options open to council members—but not the most simple acts to achieve. Flyers could be passed out until the cows come home but if people could not read what was written on them, or if they were not interested or enticed to attend the advertised community activities or events, then communication was not successful.

Those involved with the resident council (whether members or "officials") often hold disparate views about these two methods of communicating. For example, Alvin believed that knocking on doors is not always the most effective thing to do. He said:

> The mistake we've made in the past is knocking on doors just asking the basic question, "Are you interested in being on the council?" and then throwing people into a pit where they didn't realize all the things that were expected. So I hope that by this summer that we have a minimum of five people who are willing to work over in that community. I hope. Everyday my phone rings and it's always something with the council. It's, "Alvin, I just lost my job. I can't do it." "Alvin, I just cursed so and so out. I quit." Sometimes it's Jerry Springer. It's the unexpected. Something comes right out of the blue that you didn't see and, um, you grin and bear it and just move on.

Likewise, Vanessa admitted that passing out flyers could sometimes amount to information overkill. She said:

> The residents has had so many flyers stuck on their door they probably didn't know what was going on half the time. The kids would take the flyers away. It takes talking to other neighbors to let 'em know what's going on. It's really difficult to get somebody out of their comfort zone and step up to being a council member when they're not just representing their neighbors right there. They have to go up to the main office. They have to meet with other people. And some people are just shy and they don't want all that. They just want to keep very simple and very local.

On the contrary, Sharon thought the council could improve its effectiveness if its members conducted a door-to-door campaign seeking to meet and assess the needs of individual members in the community. In her words:

> Yeah. I think—um—I think if they went around and maybe polled the community to find out what they—what the community wants, what types of activities or events or benefits the community needs and wants—if they asked them and got some of their input and also ah and maybe had ah resident meeting where people could come out and learn about a resident council.

Unfortunately, the opinions of the managers, community workers, and housing authority officials do not tally with those of council members, who can speak from the perspective of once having been only residents. For example, Jessica indicated that when she first moved to Rivertown and would receive flyers about resident council meetings, she had no idea what that meant. "Well, I mean, I got the flyers and stuff," she said, "but I really didn't, you know, really understand there's a resident meeting, you know?"

Through personal interaction, Linda and Sam informed their neighbors about events and activities that were going on in Rivertown, but this method, too, seems rather small in scope. Sam expressed frustration about trying to get residents more involved. He compared it to pulling teeth:

> We sent out—every time we tried to have a resident council meeting we sent out 150 letters. If they have a problem, come to the meeting and put it on the table. We knock on the doors—ask the same thing. We come down here at 10:30 and sit in here sometimes at two o'clock maybe we may have two or maybe three and they come here then 'cause the doors open—they see the door open—but they don't come in here for the meetings and we've been trying.

The council members consistently experienced difficulty getting the adult residents involved in activities—and meetings themselves were an entirely different ball game. The only time the council meeting was packed with residents was when the housing authority officials sent out a mandatory letter telling the residents to come to the council meeting so that issues involved with a new policy could be discussed. The housing authority sent out a flyer that said:

> Dear Residents:
> A resident meeting has been scheduled for Wednesday, October 1, 2003 at 5:30pm in the Community Room of Rivertown. This is a <u>mandatory</u> meeting for any household member that is 18 years of age or older. You will be receiving up to date information concerning the Resident Survey you may have already received from HUD.
> We will be providing you with a package on *Community Service Requirements that requires your signature*. In addition, you will have the opportunity to [*sic*] here about a new Family Self-Sufficiency Program (FSS) that can help you save money that you can take advantage of right now.
>   *This is a Mandatory meeting.* Please make every effort to attend this meeting. If you fail to appear for this meeting, you will receive a letter from [*sic*]you manager requiring you to report to the Property Managers Office. Failure to comply will result in a lease violation.
>   We are looking forward to seeing you there.—Tina McVey; Housing Operations Director

Sam noted that at this meeting, with all residents present, the resident council took the opportunity to explain what the council was about. In preparation for recruiting new members or for simply cultivating volunteer help, he had even created a sign-up sheet. Some of the residents signed the sheet, but no one came to subsequent meetings. Sam said he eventually realized that the residents signed the form simply because housing authority officials were facilitating the meeting. He said:

> Like that night we helped ah when all them ah everybody had to come over here because HUD required it to sign them things so they got a community plan . . . and when I had them here then I asked everybody before everybody left all in here if anybody was interested in joining the resident council to put their name on the paper. We got a table over there and people lined up and people filled the paper—I even turned it over to the third page. And then we— I told them what time we had a meeting I said if you need—if you workin' and you get off at five o'clock you put the time down that suits you. Each one of you all put the time down that suits you. Then we'll make a meeting.

I asked him if he thought people showed up solely because they thought it would look good to the officials who would be present. To this question, Sam replied:

> Yeah I told them I said you gonna put your name on the paper—don't just do it because you 'cause we got you here now 'cause I'm gonna be coming back and looking at you when they gone and I said put the time you need the meeting to suit you and if it's not gonna suit you put down a time you think you can make the meeting.

Nobody showed.

Community dynamics, situation of the residents, and the overregulation of people in public housing has to be taken into consideration for understanding why the residents of Rivertown did not come out in droves.

RESIDENT COUNCIL MEMBERS AND LAWS AND POLICIES

In general, the council members believe the overarching HUD rules and policies with which they must abide are indeed fair. While Linda said she did not pay too much attention to them, Jessica expressed her opinion that the laws were pretty neutral and treated everybody fairly. "I think everybody is pretty much treated equally," she said. "Unless they've came up with somethin' I'm not aware of."

There is at least one notable exception to the general consensus that the laws are fair. Sam, the only African American on the council, had lived in Rivertown the longest and believed firmly that the laws were discriminatory, that they benefited those in power. He lamented the fact that people did not have a choice or voice in making the laws. "It's discriminating," he said, "because everywhere else you go you don't have to find nothing like this [such laws] here. That's discriminating." Sam tried to bring to residents a stronger awareness of the laws and policies that governed the community.

"That's why I tell the people—I said you all know what you all doin'? And they looked at me and said what you talking about," he said. "I said do you listen to the people what they tell ya? I said you don't listen, you don't listen. They could pass you anything through there." One of the rules that provoked the strongest response was the community service requirement.

COMMUNITY SERVICE REQUIREMENT
AND THE RESIDENT COUNCIL

According to the community service requirement, implemented under Section 12 of the Housing Act of 1937, as amended, every adult resident of public housing is required to perform eight hours of community service each month. This requirement does not apply to various exempted groups such as elderly persons, certain disabled individuals, and others (24 C.F.R. 960.600–609). At first the community service requirement (CSR) was required only for those communities that received a HOPE VI grant. Now, however, non–HOPE VI grant communities have to abide by the requirement as well. The managers, community workers, and housing officials perceive this new requirement in a variety of often-contradictory ways: from helpful to ineffective, equal to discriminatory.

The community service requirement affected council members differently. Linda and Sam were both exempt from it: the former, because she was on disability; the latter, because he worked. While all members of the council agreed that the new policy was a good idea in theory, they did not think that it would encourage residents to volunteer. Enforced volunteerism, they agreed, is not happy volunteerism.

The only thing Linda really knew about the new lease requirement was that able-bodied and nonworking residents were required to perform eight hours of community service a month. She thought the program provided a chance for nonworking residents to give something back to the community. She said:

> I've heard about it, but I don't know. I don't know anything about it except that you've got to do 8 hours of community service a month or something. That's about all I know. I think it's good. There's a lot of people that live here that don't have to live here. I have to live here. And there's a lot of people here that don't do anything all day, you know. They have people living in with them and they don't do anything. And the people that are on the lease, they don't do anything all day. So, you know, if they was asking you to do a lot of hours I would object. But eight hours a month, no, I wouldn't object to that. You know, some of the people don't have cars. They don't have any way of getting anywhere to do any kind of community service.

Jessica thought the requirement was a good idea but she also believed it would not do anything to alter the residents' scope of involvement in the community. "I think so many of the residents have got away with doing so much that they're not supposed to do that it's not gonna really change anything. Stuff goes on around here that shouldn't," she said. "I'll do somethin' easy. Like animals. You're not supposed to have animals, unless it's on your lease to have 'em. And people have pets and it is not on their lease. And a lot of this the landlord has known and chose to overlook it. A lot of stuff has been overlooked that's going on."

Jessica thought that the requirement would be overlooked and the residents would not be held accountable for their flouting of the rule. She did not think the new policy would convince people to join the council or help with the community. "I'd be surprised," she said, "because you know some people in the neighborhood just aren't gonna care."

Sam did not think the new requirement was fair but he understood the complexity of the new requirement and how it could hurt some and benefit others. He said:

> Nobody's gonna show up I'm telling you now. Nobody's gonna show up. Now if it's in the lease and they got to do it you gonna have somebody—they gonna show up or they gonna be out their place.

Like Jessica, Sam did not think the new requirement would increase resident council membership. "No, because see they, they can volunteer some time," he said, "but they may not volunteer for the resident council."

In general, the council members believed that while it had its positive points, the new policy also stigmatized Rivertown residents as lazy and having nothing to do; therefore, they must be *made* to be active. "Forced volunteerism," again, "is not happy volunteerism." Even the council members themselves did not fully volunteer their time, as some monetary compensation did exist, but it was not enough to separate them philosophically from those who would be forced to volunteer under the new requirement.

Community Service and Helping the Resident Council

One goal of the community service requirement was to increase membership on the resident councils. However, Sharon was not sure that residents would join the council simply because of the new policy. She said:

> It may make the council's membership grow, but once they get on the council I don't know if they'll do anything 'cause they're being forced to join something to do something and they may look at joining the council as the road of least resistance.

On the other hand, Dixie hoped that the CSR would indeed encourage residents to join the council. Volunteering in the community was something that the residents could do easily. She said:

> See they could be on the resident council and use that as community service; however, they wouldn't receive the stipend, because I know that there's a stipend that some of them receive to also participate. If they receive any kind of stipend for that or rent credit program then they—that does not count toward their community service. They cannot receive a monetary fee and then receive that same . . .

Regardless of the fact that the requirement could, in fact, increase council membership, many of the individuals interviewed for this research indicated that they had doubts about its nature and goals. Enough conflicting opinions existed about the requirement to make further investigation important.

Community Service Requirement: Discriminatory or Not?

Regarding the nature of the CSR, Alvin and Vanessa held divergent opinions. Alvin argued that the new policy wasn't discriminatory because certain people were exempted and its implementation could help the community. He saw the act as a part of the political debate. He said:

> I know a lot of our residents feel like it is punishment. Some have not said anything, but some verbally have said, "Why can't I just go about doing what I normally do" and "Why do I have to work eight hours?" "Why are you doing this to me?" So it's going to be debatable as long as the requirement stays in effect. We will always have some people who will say, "You are punishing me because I live in public housing." No, I don't think so because of the exemptions that are being given for someone the age 62 or older, someone who has a disability, someone who is working, I think it is 30 hours a week or more. If those exemptions were not in there, then I would say we've got a big problem. But all of the exemptions out there, to me, are the common sense these people should not be asked to do it.

Vanessa, however, believed the policy to be very discriminatory. She thought the eight-hour requirement was a good thing but that there was already too much government involvement in public housing. Regarding the volunteer requirement, she indicated: "I think it's good. But I think that the government is runnin' somebody's life. In order to live here, that's what you've gotta do. This is America. That's what this is, America, home of the free. Now I can't live here for free unless I volunteer for you? What do you think about that?"

In the opinion of Vanessa, HUD did not thoroughly think through who lives in public housing and what community service would mean to them.

Vanessa did not think the policies were inherently racist, but she thought they were discriminatory toward low-income people, the very audience they were meant to serve. She said:

> You're poor, but you can't live here because you've got to do this in order to live here. So that's why. There's stipulations on them, and that's another stress to add onto them. Suppose they're not capable of, or willing to do whatever that lease requires them to do? So what are they gonna do? Put 'em out and create more homelessness? And then what about your staff? That's another job task for your staff that's doing all the office procedures as it is. They're hiring people to monitor the community services on each site. That's the thing. Who's gonna monitor? And will the judge comply with the lease?

It is clear that some individuals involved in the day-to-day operation of the public housing community saw the problems inherent in the implementation of a community service requirement, but even in terms of this policy, the range of opinions they offered varied greatly. The same was true of their opinions regarding other questions involving the council: Who should lead it? Has it been successful? If not, why not?

HUD expected that resident councils would be active agents for community building. The expectation stemmed from the past history of housing laws and policies that purposefully discriminated, segregated, and isolated African Americans in housing and public housing. This history was further exacerbated by HUD's mismanagement of funds and poor construction of public housing. Adding to this mix were external structural factors that affected the African American community: changes in the global community, outmigration of middle-class African- Americans to the suburbs, changing attitudes toward race and race relations.

Using CRT illuminates the historical context that shaped public housing policies. CRT also identifies that if we do not address the history of housing laws and policies, understand the assumptions or "single truths" behind the racialization of housing laws, take into account the narratives of individuals who live in public housing, and comprehend how their realities are shaped by housing laws and policies, inequality and disjuncture will persist.

Resident council laws and policies did not take into account the community dynamics or the bevy of social service agencies that had an impact, not only on the council members' daily lives but also on how members connected and became involved in the Rivertown Resident Council. Resident council laws and policies also did not take into account the racialized assumptions and stereotypes of those who were interpreting, implementing, and enforcing those laws and policies.[5]

HUD and HA laws and regulations required that council members attend a certain number of meetings beyond their regular council sessions. Such laws and policies also dictated the proper way of electing an official resident council and established the form a resident meeting should take. The council members thought there were too many meetings, and they agreed that they often felt they received nothing from attending the extra ones, during which they generally did not speak or participate fully. Advertising and communication of meeting information not only to the council but to the residents was another problem with the meeting structures. The resident council members were not able to get the residents involved in council meetings or activities, despite their hard work to inform the community. Methods of communication were affected by the predetermined assumptions of managers, housing authority officials, and community workers about the council and residents and the policies and actions of management.

NOTES

1. Winton Park, West Chester, Forest Park, and Oakland are pseudonyms for the different public housing communities in the city.

2. Public housing reform is represented through the Quality Housing and Work Responsibility Act of 1998 (QHWRA). QHWRA was signed by President Clinton on October 21, 1998, and is found in Title V of HUD's FY1999 appropriations act (Pub. L. No. 105-276). QHWRA is landmark legislation that will make public housing reform a reality by (1) reducing the concentration of poverty in public housing; (2) protecting access to housing assistance for the poorest families; (3) supporting families making the transition from welfare to work; (4) raising performance standards for public housing agencies, and rewarding high performance; (5) transforming the public housing stock through new policies and procedures for demolition and replacement and mixed-finance projects, and through authorizing the HOPE VI revitalization program; (6) merging and reforming the Section 8 certificate and voucher programs, and allowing public housing agencies to implement a Section 8 homeownership program Supporting HUD management reform efficiencies through deregulation and streamlining and program consolidation.

3. In contrast, resident councils sometimes become involved in their communities when their homes are being affected by demolition or environmental issues. Examples of active resident councils would be the St. Thomas public housing community of New Orleans. Also, several lawsuits have been filed from resident council members to stop the physical threat to their homes such as: *Little Earth of United Tribes, Inc. v. United States Dep't of Housing & Urban Dev* (1983); *Cabrini-Green Advisory Council v. Chicago Housing Authority* (1997); *Resident Council of Allen Parkway Village v. United States Dep't of Housing & Urban Development* (1993), and *Alexandria Resident Council, Inc., v. Alexandria Redevelopment & Housing Authority* (2003).

4. Although the focus of the council was on the children, they still wanted the parents and community members to be involved and get suggestions for having activities and events for the children. They also wanted to know of any concerns of the residents, and they wanted them to come to the meetings.

5. That is, managers, housing authority officials, and community workers.

Chapter Six

Meetings and Manager Dynamics

Organizing and attending meetings was a major job requirement of the resident council. Meetings are stressed in the *Code of Federal Regulations*, bylaws, and the Green Book. The policies articulate how the resident council members should have control of the meetings, how they should meet regularly, and how they should involve the community. Nonetheless, the requirements and expectations of meetings and the reality of them were another area of disjunction. Numerous factors contributed to this disjunction.

One factor was a disconnect between who the rules state should be running the meetings and who actually was. Various rules specify that the resident council members should be in charge of their own meetings. However, the members were often divested of their promised "ownership" in the meetings. When housing authority members or managers attended meetings, the council members' voices tended to get silenced. Another factor was the frequency of "extra" meetings. The housing officials wanted council members to attend meetings and be a part of the decision-making process. They wanted them to be involved; therefore, regular attendance was urged, both at the resident council meetings and at others. Consistent with this view, the resident council members usually had no problems attending their own council meetings. However, attendance at other meetings was more problematic for them. Resident council members often felt that at such "extra" meetings as the joint resident council meetings, nothing got done, so they resented having to take time off from work or find a babysitter in order to attend. Finally, not being able to communicate effectively with residents hampered the council's ability to engage in community building. These and other problems are described in more detail below.

ORGANIZING AND HOLDING REGULAR MEETINGS

In the Rivertown Council Bylaws, Article VII: Meetings sets forth the rules for organizing and holding regular meetings:

> The Council must organize and attend at least one regularly scheduled month-ly meeting of the Resident Council, and one regularly scheduled monthly event which is open to all residents. The event which is open to all residents must be well publicized. Sign in sheets should be collected at both meetings.
>
> At least one elected representative must attend the regularly scheduled Site Based Planning Meeting which is organized and facilitated by the Manager.
>
> Additional meetings may be called by any elected representative, however other representatives are not obligated to attend without at least 48 hours' notice.

In addition to their own meetings, council members had to attend sessions organized by the housing authority, identified as site-based and as joint resident council sessions.

MEETING TYPES

Council members had to attend three different types of meetings: weekly resident council meetings,[1] once-a-month site-based meetings, and once-a-month joint resident council meetings. I will briefly discuss the dynamics of the three types of meetings that resident council members had to attend.

Regular Resident Council Meetings

The regular meetings formed the heart of the resident council; the meetings were controlled by members, and it was during these meetings that decisions were made. Council members set the meeting schedule: initially, they met every Monday at 6:00 p.m., but eventually—to accommodate schedules and encourage greater attendance—they switched to Fridays at 10:30 a.m. Based upon this schedule, then, the council should have met four times a month. The number and regularity of meetings would increase depending on the activities and events planned. At first the meetings were held in the community room, but then the meetings were moved to the resident council office in the community center.

Before I attended my first resident council meeting, I assumed the session would be organized similar to the other meetings of groups and organizations to which I belong. For instance, at my monthly sorority meeting, everyone signed an attendance sheet, reviewed an agenda, and discussed the minutes from the last meeting. Once the president called the meeting to order, some-one (usually the elected secretary) took minutes, and we could all expect to be able to voice our concerns and opinions. Such a meeting followed the tenets set forth in *Robert's Rules of Order*, the established "bible" for conducting efficient, effective meetings.

The first council meetings I attended followed similar procedures. There was a sign-in sheet, an agenda was distributed, and someone wrote down the minutes. Jane was always there to ensure that the event followed "meeting procedure."

Who's Running the Meeting?

One area of disjunction between the stated policies and the realities of the resident council is the answer to the question "Who's running the meeting?" Although the resident council members were clearly supposed to run their own meetings, this was not always the case. My observations at Rivertown indicated that the structure of the resident council meeting would vary depending upon the presence of individuals who were not members. There is nothing in the Green Book on rules to indicate that the structure of a meeting should vary as a result of non–resident council members being present. Being self-sufficient involves taking ownership of one's own meeting, even with housing authority officials in attendance. However, such was not the case with the resident council meetings I observed. I noticed major differences when the regular meetings were run by the resident council members without Jane or Vanessa being present, as compared to when they were there. I knew that these meetings were supposed to be run by the resident council members and that Jane's job was merely to help them get organized, but this was not the case. It was easy to notice a discernible power imbalance. Even though the Green Book stresses that "resident council should be run by the residents," that obviously was not always the case. At council meetings not attended by Jane or Vanessa, there was an equal distribution of power among members.

Council Meetings as Esteem Boosters and Social Events

In spite of the changing dynamics (new members, managers, and housing authority officials) of the council, the active resident council members told me that they enjoyed coming to the meetings. Attending the meetings was an esteem booster, but it also provided a chance for social gathering, as several members indicated. In Linda's opinion, for example, attending the meetings boosted her self-esteem. She indicated that "when I'd go down there [to the council meetings] I would feel pretty good about myself, about what I was accomplishing."

Jessica indicated that she enjoyed going to the meetings because it got her out of the house and provided a period of time when she could be sociable with other adults. She said, "I enjoyed getting out of the house, definitely.

Doing somethin' with my time and goin' down there and it was a time for me to be social with everybody."

Sam said he liked attending the meetings because he felt that the other members of the council were his family. In addition, he enjoyed the outcomes the meetings would produce. He said: "Hey, 'cause it's fun and I tell you when I see them kids like ah just last Friday when all them kids' face lit up when all this food and stuff hey that makes joy." He even appreciated those members who did not show up on a regular basis and other residents in the community who did not become involved. "Hey, the ones not on the resident council? I like them, too. They still my family."

All who routinely attended meetings agreed that the time spent at the council sessions were enjoyable because they provided an opportunity to socialize, a chance to establish goals, and a period of time wherein they felt they were working toward the common goal of helping the community's children. At other regular meetings, council members shared recipes, talked about good mechanics in the area, touched on church and God, discussed the police, and commented on children in the community. During such meetings, members were able to build social ties and network among each other. They were, in essence, their own support group that sometimes provided resources and links to a larger network . The importance of social ties and networking as a necessary ingredient for people to work together toward a common interest is well established (Lin 2001; Portes 1998; Coleman 1988; Putnam 1993, 1995; Bourdieu 1986). Furthermore, research indicates that social networking and community involvement and the social interactions resulting from groups and associations improve levels of life satisfaction, increase personal health, and generate societal and government trust (Hawe and Shiel 2000; Kaase 1999). What resident council members lost in efficiency may well have been a fair trade for what they gained.

Although the council members at times faulted Maynard or Alvin for not attending meetings regularly, it does appear that they enjoyed those meetings most that were unattended by any "officials." At such meetings, they were able to relax and be themselves. Moreover, although they did not follow strict parliamentary procedures, on such occasions that council members got down to planning activities on their own, they seemed more empowered and capable.

In my time with the council, they showed stability and flexibility, consistency and inconsistency, and group cohesion and group disarray. In that time there were multiple changes in HUD rules and policies, and three managers, two people from the housing authority, and two community workers who worked directly with the resident council. Out of the nine duly elected resident council members, only three were truly active members.

Site-Based Meetings

Site-based meetings occurred at 10:30 a.m. on the second Wednesday of each month. The meetings were held in the Rivertown Community Center and involved the resident council, manager, maintenance personnel, and any out-side community service providers who had been invited and chose to attend. During such meetings, issues, questions, and concerns were addressed to the community.

Recounting the things that property managers should be doing, Maynard told me that one of their duties was to hold such site-based meetings. He said:

> There are things that property managers should be doing that they're not doing. Each month, every property manager is supposed to hold a site-based meeting. Which includes community service providers, the resident council, and maintenance to address issues in their communities.

When I asked him if the managers had to do it, he responded:

> Yes, it's a requirement from HUD. And that's the area in which the resident councils will tell either maintenance or the property manager or both of them, the residents are having these issues. I have residents that put in a work order to have a window fixed three months ago and, you know, it hasn't been fixed yet. What's going on? But because the property manager isn't holding that meeting, then the residents don't have a venue to inform them of the concerns in the community.

Discussing a good time to have a site-based meeting, Dixie informed me of her role at the meeting and the importance of site-based meetings in general. She said:

> We need a site-based meeting date so that I can do minutes, we can hash out any issues that I need to be addressed with at that meeting and then the resident council if that's a good time for them they can keep having it. But, the other three meetings in the month are for the resident council and I'm not going to be involved in those, but what I'm going to do at that point is take those site-based minutes and also let Alvin look at those and see if anything he needs to address and help with too.

Joint Resident Council

The joint resident council meeting occurred the second Thursday of every month. The meeting usually started at 6:00 p.m. These meetings consisted of resident council members from the area's other public housing communities. At these meetings the discussion revolved around the housing authority and the issues in all of the local public housing communities. Besides representa-tives from the resident councils, the executive directors from the housing authority attended, as did some managers and community service workers. I attended four of the joint resident council meetings. Daniel defined these meetings, which were also known as the president's advisory board:

> One of the things that we actually do is have a president's advisory meeting which is held at least once a month. And that's the president of all the resident councils. And we actually hold those meetings [the housing authority], and at different times we're invited to come to those meetings for specific reasons. At one time we had a staff that actually held this meeting. Right now that's being held by one staff person on the Resolution Action Center staff.
>
> One might imagine that with all of the rules that govern the workings of the resident council and the responsibilities of the housing authority officials, community workers, and managers, as well as all of the opportunities given council members to meet either in their small groups or with other concerned councils, the pathway to successful planning and implementation of activities was clear, this is not the case. In fact, the Rivertown Resident Council was not meeting HUD expectations for the council as an active agent for community building.

SOCIAL SERVICE CAROUSEL

Resident council members had to deal with a bevy of issues beyond just living in public housing: money, child support, health, employment, and child care. As stated earlier, issues of economic inequality or poverty did not stand alone. The managers, community workers, and housing authority officials were fully aware of such issues and how they affected the council members and residents in general. Members of the council had to deal also with the social service carousel in one form or another—public housing itself being one form.

In this section I argue that housing officials were aware of these problems, but ignored them in several ways. If council members' lived experiences were taken into consideration, then they would not have to adhere to a community service requirement or other restrictive policies that were deemed by some as "punishments." Even if HUD officials were aware of the strains and stresses that residents have to deal with, they still had to enforce applicable policies. The number of meetings and other requirements imposed by housing officials on the council members were another way they demonstrated their lack of sensitivity to the council. In addition, housing officials attributed the lack of effective community-building activities as personal failures and not as a result of the problems encountered by the resident council members.

Alvin was aware of the range of multiple issues encountered by residents in public housing. He was not blind to the fact that joining a resident council was on the low end of the priority list for a lot of the residents. He said:

I think if Alvin stepped back and said, "I'm just going to see what these folks are going to do," that nothing would happen. Absolutely nothing. And I say that because for every person, whether it's two elderly sites or our seven family developments, there are so many other issues on their plate, this is for many just kind of like a hangnail. "I'll get to it when I get to it." I would have them work on another service side so they can see just some of the struggles that our folks are dealing with. Because it's huge. So many of my caseload families, the ladies weren't receiving any help with child care or with anything.

Alvin also noted that there were many demands and requirements placed on these people and that if they did not fulfill them, they could get sanctioned. He said:

And that is why, as good as the philosophy and the concept of the resident council is, I've just been a firm believer that if we are not meeting the needs of our residents and they're dealing with those other issues, I mean, it's . . . There are a lot of things on my plate that I put at the very bottom because they're not pressing needs, and our residents are the same way. And for many the resident council falls right at the bottom because of those other pressing issues that they're facing. They don't have medical insurance. They don't have dental insurance. Their children are struggling in school. They can't be an advocate because they're uncomfortable talking to the teacher because they last time they went to meet with the teacher the teacher used education and talked down to them. I mean, it's all of those things that they're facing. So when they see a notice on their door that says, "Resident Meeting tonight at 7:00" they're like, "Please."

Alvin said that the living situations in Rivertown were not so bad, not so drastic—and that this fact itself might make membership in the council seem less important. Currently, there is not a "pressing need" in the community for people to take action. "When people reach that point of 'Hmmm, hmmm, hmmm' then it's just . . . But when they hit someone or someone's child is killed because of a drug deal, or a kid gets hit by a car because people are speeding through, that one issue is enough for people who get together to just say 'enough,'" he noted.

Because of budget cuts, Daniel discussed how important it was for social service agencies to help residents in the public housing community. If the other agencies helped, council members could become more self-sufficient. He said:

Oh, it would be nice if they could be. It would be nice. It would take a lot more staff to try to push a program like that. You know, most housing authorities, right now, because of budget cuts and things, most housing authorities have on-staff property managers. People can manage the development. But as far as doing other programs, you have to kind of depend on other agencies you can

refer people to. But in Lincoln, we have staff over at Lincoln that specifically
work with self-sufficiency. Which makes a difference.

Despite being aware of the multitude of issues that individuals face in
public housing, officials still required resident council members to attend
several "outside" meetings and looked down upon members when they were
deemed to be less active in council activities. When individuals failed to
become involved with the council, or when their involvement waned, housing officials tended to interpret them as "being lazy or having a lack of
leadership," but the behavior might be caused quite easily by a number of
divergent life factors: lack of child care, an inability to take a day off from
work, and the like.

With regard to what I deem the "social service carousel," Vanessa had a
lot to say, particularly regarding the dynamics of living in public housing, the
services that are in place to help, and the government policies with which
individuals must deal. She provided an interesting analysis of people's perception regarding the residents and the social service agencies with which
they dealt, but her insight still labeled residents of public housing as children.
She said:

> People in public housing are far better than people out in the public sector
> because, if I lose my job first of all I have to hustle to find a job. I may not
> make as much money as I made before, I have a house note I have to pay, let's
> say rent because it's probably a big rent. So something is going to suffer. Will
> I know . . . Will I lower my pride and come to the Presbyterian Center to get
> food? Will I go down and apply for food stamps? I don't think so. We would
> suffer, my children will suffer.
>
> If you live in public housing you don't have to worry about heat, you don't
> have to worry about calling a plumber to fix your toilet. We have a mainte-
> nance staff here on-site. You don't have to worry about the light bill being
> paid. People in Section 8 can't make the bills and that's why they come here.

In 1996, President William Clinton signed into law the Personal Responsibility and Work Opportunity Reconciliation Act (PRWORA). This major
reform bill replaced Aid to Families with Dependent Children (AFDC) with
Temporary Aid to Needy Families (TANF). TANF differed from AFDC in
that it included a mandatory work requirement; provided time-limited cash
assistance; and offered incentives for remaining married, reducing nonmarital pregnancies, and living in two-parent households (Fitzgerald and Ribar
2004; Huang 2002; Gooden and Bailey 2001). Once again we see how racialized and class-based stigmas regarding the poor carry over into policies and
laws.

POWER POSITION OF THE HOUSING MANAGER

An area of disjunction related to the manager involves the dynamics of power. The housing manager[2] possesses the resources and influence to help the council achieve its desired outcomes and goals for the community. In essence, the manager is in a position of power "to make decisions having major consequences" (Mills 1956) for the council, in both positive and negative terms. Even with all the laws and policies that empower the resident council, the relationship between the manager and council still is power dependent. If council members do not know how much power they have or even what their rights might be, they can be pawns for the manager. As Emerson (1962, 32) states, "power resides implicitly in the other's dependency." Addressing the issue of power, critical race theory stresses that without taking into account the lived experiences of individuals to ensure equality in the law, the construction and implementation of laws and policies are appropriated as "hegemonic devices" that in essence protect the power of the dominant group (Jay 2003, 3).

Alvin, Sharon, Dixie, and Maynard described the effect the power of the manager can have on the council. Alvin agreed that managers have a powerful effect on the resident council. He said:

> I've seen some communities that don't have a resident council. The impact is because the manager has not pushed it. When I came on board in June, there were three councils that were considered inactive. So somewhere along the way that manager has either verbally or nonverbally given the impression that if you have one it's great, if you don't have one it's great.

Sharon also agreed that the manager's support can shape the inactivity or activity of the council:

> I think that any resident council needs the support of the manager—needs to have the manager's backing and support, if they have a manager. Like, for instance, like there's several maybe two communities that I can think off top that the manager is not very supportive of the resident council and they actively work, not against them, but they don't do anything to help them so they have really been struggling for a long time.

In other words, not having a council or supporting a council that does exist is a way a manager can maintain control over the community. Sharon continued with her point:

> I know another community that the manager is not very active at all in trying to get the resident council started. It's a struggling community. They have never had a resident council that's been really effective. It's always been struggling whenever they get like one or two people on it, but I think that's

because the manager doesn't really ah—I don't know if they want a resident council in that particular community, because then it's going to put pressure on them to do the things that they need to do.

Dixie and Maynard reported having witnessed incidents where managers had taken control, dominated the council, and then used it for their own personal gain, instead of for the betterment or the "enhancing" of the community it was meant to represent. Discussing examples of how managers have run resident councils, thus defeating the very reasons for their existence, Dixie indicated that

> management has run the resident council meeting and that's not what it's meant for it's meant for them to run and we need to just get their input and be of assistance if I can. But, it's not, you know—the site-based meetings to run and handle what goes on there but the resident council meeting is the resident council meeting it's for residents.

Maynard suggested that while overly controlling managers can prove detrimental to resident councils, those who practice a "hands-off" policy and withhold support can be equally problematic. If threatened, a manager can keep resident council members and residents in the dark about the council or use it to his or her benefit, which flies in the face of CFR regulations, the mission and operation statement of the housing authorities, and the role of the manager to (as the job description indicates) "work closely with resident councils as an advisor on housing matters." Instead of having an active council, such managers create what Maynard calls a mannequin resident council:

> We have neighborhoods that have property managers that support their resident council, because they understand that an effective resident council is in fact a help to them. We have other property managers who are not doing what they're supposed to be doin', so they don't want a strong resident council to pull their coattail and tell them, look, you're not doin' what you're supposed to be doin'. So, you know, some of them have what I call mannequin resident councils. You know, it looks like a resident council, you know, it wears clothes just like a council would, but it's not functioning. It's just a window dressing. And the managers manipulate those councils to either get back at certain residents they don't like. They use those councils to police the neighborhood. They use those councils to do things they're not comfortable doing. And a lot of the things that some of these councils are doing it's not their responsibility to do. It's the responsibility of those property managers. Um, and then you have property managers that don't want no form, shape, or fashion of a resident council to take place. Just because they don't want them to even trip up on their rights. They don't want them to stumble upon their rights as a resident council.

The managerial position is such a powerful one that the individual who assumes one can, if he or she chooses, control and exploit council members. Under such circumstances, the function of the council can often be distorted: as previously noted, its members can be viewed variously as snitches, police agents, or "manager's pets."

Alvin noted that there are no policies, evaluations, pay increases, or repercussions in place that would influence the manager to create, maintain, and support an active resident council. He indicated:

> There's nothing major that would cause or influence a manager to say, "I'm going to get five people and go ahead and get a resident council goin' because if I don't my pay or my evaluation is going to get deducted ten points." No. But what I try to sell the managers on, look at our communities that have what I consider to be effective resident councils.

Alvin's assertion is supported by the managerial evaluation. The eight-page performance evaluation form provided by the Ridgeway Housing Authority for management personnel to complete does not address the manager's support of the resident council. The topics for evaluation include:

Program activities
Budgetary development and control activities
Investigation and evaluation activities
Supervisory/managerial activities
Operational awareness activities
Policy formulation activities
Cooperative activities

The support and involvement of the manager with the council could possibly fit under managerial activities, policy formulation activities, or cooperative activities, but information regarding such is not asked for overtly. In effect, as a subject, resident council involvement is missing from the evaluation form. Since the CFR and HUD strongly encourage and support resident councils, one would think that manager's involvement would be a category for evaluation.

DIFFERENCE IN ENFORCEMENT AND IMPLEMENTATION OF POLICIES

Another area of disjunction involves the enforcement and implementation of policies. In the beginning, the housing authority supported the managerial style adopted by Vanessa, but as policies and rules changed, so too did the housing authority's approach to the residents and council members. Vanessa had been with the Ridgeway Housing Authority for over ten years, working for an agency that is directly affected and monitored by government policies and laws and budget cuts. In her time with the housing authority, she witnessed the election of two presidents, the 1993 passage of the Government Performance and Results Act (GPRA) requiring all federally funded agencies to develop and implement an accountability system based on performance measurements, the development by HUD of new strategic goal and planning objectives, and the enacting of public housing reforms laws, such as the Quality Housing and Work Responsibility Act of 1998 (QHWRA). As the Ridgeway Housing Authority experienced changes due to these factors, so did Vanessa—and by necessity she was forced to change her managerial style. For instance, the informal practice of having teenagers or residents volunteer in the office was against policy, so it had to be abandoned. According to Dixie, "The information in the office is confidential, so they cannot be going through the filing and work with it."

One of the new strategic goals enacted by HUD is designed to help families and individuals become economically self-sufficient. Programs, grants, and policies supported and strongly encouraged by HUD and the housing authority include the Family Self-Sufficiency Program (FSSP), Resident Opportunities and Self Sufficiency Program (ROSS), and the Welfare to Work Voucher Program (WtW). Vanessa supported these programs, but she was also aware of the barriers, stresses, and emotions that individuals go through trying to "get on their feet." In her time as manager, Vanessa saw her efforts to get to know residents and to provide them with someone in whom they could place their trust as a method of helping the whole person. Stressful environmental conditions, such as living in public housing, influence parenting strategies (Ceballo and McLoyd 2002; Hashima and Amato 1994), social support (Keating-Lefler et al. 2004), and mental and physical health (Leventhal and Brooks-Gunn 2003), and these factors in turn affect people's ability to leave public housing or deal with the barrage of social service agencies. By turning a sympathetic ear or providing a friendly face, Vanessa attempted to overcome these problems and connect with the residents. She made this assessment about people living in public housing:

> Unfortunately in public housing your residents aren't working. They don't have careers. They don't have jobs. So they are at home and they have serious barriers that they need to discuss with someone and if you are calling them, talking to social services, and you don't have anybody on the phone to speak with concerning your problems, then you're somewhat limited. So if there was an opportunity for them to come and discuss some of their problems with me, then that's what they did in order to even get the rent.

From the first time I met her until the day she left, Vanessa always had piles and piles of folders stacked across her desk. These piles never got smaller. I would wonder how she ever got the paperwork done because she was always helping the residents. At one point, I asked her if she had an office manager, and she said that she did not. I later found out that Dixie used to be her office manager but that she was, in fact, stationed at a location away from Rivertown. Currently, Dixie, the new manager, has an office manager with her at Rivertown. Dixie, in fact, said she would get killed by the paperwork that Vanessa passed along to her. Since Vanessa focused on the residents more so than her other managerial duties, she did not always have the best evaluations. Reflecting on her evaluations, she said:

> It was divided into different portions. And my evaluations were different each year, depending on who that supervisor was. I never really had any positive, maybe one or two really good evaluations. But they weren't always bad, either. Maybe one or two in the 10 years I was there. Maybe one or two stinky ones that I didn't particularly care for.

Despite not always having the best evaluations or receiving "rewards" from the "company," she still persisted in her efforts to do things for the residents. It was from the residents, in fact, that she received her biggest rewards and greatest satisfaction:

> Yeah, but, you know, you really don't get your rewards from the company, from the housing authority. It depends on your supervisor and towards the end we had a pretty decent supervisor who understood what we did and how we did it. She actually did the work that we did as a housing manager. But you got your appreciation from your residents when you succeed the results of something you helped assist them with.

Without question, Vanessa had passion for her job. She realized that in order to be an effective manager, one must balance working with residents and maintaining managerial duties, but she refused to compromise her "motherly" managerial style. With regard to this style and to other managers, she noted:

> That's where the management style comes in. If you're good at doing office management, pushing the paper, then you're not gonna be equally as good at working with residents. So you gotta understand, what would be your role? My role was working with people. I'm a people-oriented manager, not an office manager pushing paper. And that's the style I chose to keep. So I mean you can't expect some like Dixie to come in and manage . . . her expertise is not in property management. She's an administrative assistant. She's always done paperwork. Can you imagine? She has no personality at all with people.

Perhaps the best type of manager must be able to balance heart with managerial effectiveness. Every manager is different and possesses his or her own unique style. Whatever style of managing is chosen, however, will inevitably influence the operation and goals of the resident council.

VANESSA AND THE RIVERTOWN COUNCIL:
A DIFFERENCE IN RESPONSIBILITIES

Since Vanessa was a people person, she was extremely involved with the Resident Council—so much so, in fact, that her overzealous passion often led her, perhaps unintentionally, to become controlling and dominating. In her opinion, it was her job to bring the council together, to be its leader, and to recruit members to it. Doing so, she believed, would make the council more effective and help bring about positive change within the community. As stated in the CFR, Ridgeway's mission and operation statement, and even in her job description, though, this level of interaction with and control over the council were beyond the parameters outlined for her role as manager. Even having the best intentions for the council can lead to disjunction if the manager's focus is not centered on the council's desires and if policies for assisting the council are ignored. Her passion for the people and helping the resident council became a motive behind her drive of leadership and power over the council (Fox 2000).

In the discipline of business and management, Vanessa's adoption of a "leadership role" would not be acceptable because she not was trying to integrate and balance the needs and goals of the "stakeholders" (Jaffee 2001; Lloyd 1996). Her methodology seemed to involve an exertion of superior force rather than a true leadership approach that would motivate, inspire, and stimulate constant improvements (Bryman, Stephens, and Campo 1996; Avolio and Bass 1995).

Yet, people at the housing authority were surprised that when Vanessa left Rivertown, the formerly active, strong council basically disintegrated. Dixie reported her own response: "I was really surprised; because . . . it was my understanding that Vanessa was really strong at keeping these people involved in their community." Even Vanessa had trouble understanding why the council fell apart after she left:

> Well, it was effective. You were there long enough to see that it did work. And it shouldn't have fallen apart when I left. It should have stayed there. It should have stayed together. That's why you try not to have one person in charge. And they didn't have a president per se. When you volunteer to do something, every group has a leader. Somebody to lead and guide them. That's just the way life is. I had a wonderful resident council and I kept them together when there was a conflict. We tried to work those things out.

In fact, Linda herself joined the council because Vanessa talked to her about it. This example indicates that the manager's efforts at recruitment can be positive. However, the experience can turn out negatively as well. For example, Vanessa also recruited Lucy, who later turned out to be a bad fit for the council and council members. Because Vanessa was more persistent with some of the people she recruited than with others, primarily due to skills they possessed that she imagined could be put to use by the council, rumors began to circulate that the council members were being handpicked by her. Somehow, this rumor spread to other housing authority officials. Dixie told me that some residents "were told they couldn't be on the resident council." I cannot, however, verify this, as during the time I spent at Rivertown, I observed only that Vanessa attempted to get people involved and to assist them in any way she could.

How councils were formed in the past also might have affected recruitment efforts over time. As Vanessa noted:

> Well, at one point in time we had a department whose position was specifically designed to form resident councils. However, people are creatures of habit and if they don't really know you, you've got to have a winning personality to get people to give their time as a volunteer to be a community leader. That takes a lot of work. A lot of work. But as property manager, I knew the people, you know, who was working and who's not working and you just know these things that other folks don't know, because it's like a big family. You know everything about these people.

The example of Vanessa indicates the degree to which opinions and responses were divided with regard to the degree of involvement even a relatively successful manager—one with clearly evolved people skills who cared for the members of her community—should have with the council. Since the manager assumes a level of power within the community, to have that individual participate in the council is to alter its potential dynamics.

NOTES

1. Bylaws said resident councils should meet once a month, but they decided to have weekly meetings instead.
2. I use housing manager and property manager interchangeably.

Chapter Seven

Policy Recommendations

My research shows that seven obstacles stand in the way of the desired relationship between the resident council and the HUD officials: (1) emphasis on children, (2) leadership of the council, (3) perception that the resident council members are "snitches," (4) responsibilities of the resident council and HUD officials, (5) manager/ managerial styles, (6) meeting dynamics, and (7) HUD structure and priorities.

Using critical race theory to explain the seven disjunctions, we find that the interpretation, implementation, and enforcement of resident council laws and policies (1) minimize the experiences and knowledge of individuals who live in public housing and (2) do not take into account race and the intersection of multiple status characteristics. These two factors create a false assumption of color blindness and maintain a system of racial inequality perpetuated by the housing authority officials, community workers, and managers. Such officials often hold negative assumptions and stereotypes about public housing and the people who live there, and because of these assumptions, the same officials tend to overlook, marginalize, or minimize the intersectionality[1] of people's lived experiences.

Given the earlier discussion, two major tasks can be identified that would help reduce, and in some cases, eliminate the obstacles confronting the Rivertown Resident Council:

1. Leadership development training must be undertaken for the managers, housing authority officials, community workers, and resident council.
2. Resource development must occur for managers, housing authority officials, and community workers.

In the next section I give a broad overview of the two tasks, then I discuss how the tasks could help reduce each of the seven disjunctions.

LEADERSHIP DEVELOPMENT TRAINING

Leadership development training (LDT) has been used in the fields of business, management, government agencies, health care, and nonprofit organizations.[2] As the name implies, LDT helps individuals develop leadership skills, skills that in turn help improve their organization.

Since residents and resident council members are meant to be valuable stakeholders and clients in public housing, then they must be treated as such. The fact that such individuals live in public housing and are often enmeshed in the social service system should not deter managers, housing authority officials, or community workers from treating them with respect and dignity—as all clients should be treated. Although housing officials no doubt have had training and experience, I argue that more could be done to help them interact with this specialized clientele in ways that are free of negative assumptions about race, public housing, class, or poverty. Housing officials need additional training so that they can conceptualize the personal experiences of the resident council members as valuable assets while being sensitive to the reality that these same experiences often present major hurdles for the members. Changes in job descriptions and additional and ongoing training for housing officials would be beneficial. Specifically, HUD officials[3] must create and require attendance at various training workshops that address such issues as professionalism, leadership, networking, communication, and diversity / cultural competency skills.

Professionalism

The housing authority officials, managers, and community workers face numerous demands that require for their successful completion a variety of complex and interrelated abilities and skills. For example, Alvin told me that his job specified a need for someone who worked with the Ridgeway population but was also a service provider in the city. The job descriptions of Maynard and Sharon asked for individuals with excellent interpersonal and group process skills who could provide leadership, mentoring, and group problem-solving assistance. However, once hired, no on-the-job training was provided. For instance, when Jane was hired, she said she did not receive any training but had to learn by "just doing." Dixie moved from office manager to property manager all in one year. This "in the trenches" style of learning the crucial skills associated with the job means that often individuals are not trained in the social science profession. To remedy this, the housing authority must hire more qualified staff to address the needs of the individuals who live in Rivertown. I suggest that a qualified, professional staff should have at least a bachelor's or master's degree in a related field such as social work, sociology, public health, or human development. This individual should also possess other skills that would enable him or her to address efficiently and with particular insight the specialized needs of public housing residents. In fact, the moniker "professional" implies certain prerequisites for those who hold it:

- The provision of service affecting the health, well-being and/or safety of society,
- Appropriate certification or licensing,
- A rigorous academic background,
- Personal accountability to both the state and either national or statewide professional association performance standards, and
- A large measure of autonomy (McNamara 2004)

If the Ridgeway Housing Authority cannot afford to hire professional individuals, then they should consider securing a consultant who will be responsible for training the managers and housing authority officials in the appropriate professional skills. In order to provide the best possible service to its clients, the Ridgeway Housing Authority should reevaluate the criteria and qualifications it has established for the various positions it oversees.

Developing Professional Guidelines

Currently there are no training manuals, workshops, or peer-mentoring guides in place at the Ridgeway Housing Authority. This suggests that the housing authority has not defined or established specific roles and goals for people who work under its charge. In fact, the role of the housing authority officials is loosely defined in the CFR. The Ridgeway Housing Authority does not have any specific manuals that address or define officials' roles and job responsibilities to the council. By creating such a manual, the housing authority could clarify its expectations for housing officials and then make sure that staff members receive proper training for their roles and responsibilities to the residents and the resident council. Just as HUD possesses a strategic plan for its agency, the Ridgeway Housing Authority needs to develop a similar plan, one that would focus on how its agents could better establish client relationships.

The content of the strategic planning process depends on the needs of the community and its immediate external environment. However, the resident council members, residents, and current housing authority staff should participate in developing the strategic plan. For example, in an organization whose services change rapidly, planning should be carried out frequently. Since there is a high turnover rate among employees at the housing authority and among residents at the complex itself, then the strategic plan should reflect such changes. The strategic plan for Rivertown might cover the following subjects:

1. Strategizing goals and methods / strategies to achieve goals,
2. Identifying strategic directions,
3. Identifying strengths, weaknesses, opportunities, and threats (SWOT analysis),
4. Developing/updating a values statement,
5. Action planning: defining objectives, responsibilities, timeline,
6. Methods for writing and communicating the plan, and
7. Monitoring, evaluating, and deviating from the plan (McNamara 2004)

The position of manager clearly seems to require service both as a social worker and a property manager, but these requirements do not come close to describing the multitude of tasks that such an individual must perform. A strategic plan could help provide direction and focus for the manager. Then, once the strategic plan is developed, more informed hiring decisions can be made and the appropriate training plans can be developed. For example, given the importance of grants described in this book, hiring someone with grant-writing ability might be a top priority. Alternatively, the housing authority must also determine whether it would be willing to train a particular individual for the position if that person lacks any of the prerequisite skills, such as grant writing, but is in other ways a "good match" for the job. Should the decision be undertaken to train the manager, housing authority officials must then determine the length of training, the funds required for such training, and how the delay caused by the training would impact residents.

In addition, professional development would require mentoring. Browne-Ferrigno and Muth (2004, 469) state that professional leadership "involves more than just recruitment, preparation, licensure, and placement. It involves an ongoing evaluation and supervision and coaching and continuous career long professional development."

Outside Consultant or Facilitator

Perhaps the most certain way to ensure that changes occur at Rivertown is through the hiring of a consultant or facilitator from outside the organization—someone with no ties to HUD—who will assist in the establishment and meeting of goals. Currently, Maynard and Sharon act as outside facilitators for Rivertown, but they are funded through HUD grant monies and, as a result, have an obligation to the housing authority.

Several outside agencies could provide such a consultant for Rivertown. For example, such companies as Lominger Limited Inc., Jim Kouzes, and Barry Posner specialize in leadership training and team building. Training could also come from the state. For example, the Department of Social Services has a state-trained coordinator whose position requires visiting various social service departments and assessing how they deal with difficult situations. It is this consultant's job to train state employees to deal with any difficult situation, whether internal, external, or both. The housing authority could request that a state coordinator for social services assist with on-site development of leadership, professional, and communication skills—in effect, to train HUD officials[4] so they can be more attuned to the lived experiences of the council members and residents of Rivertown. As a central part of their evaluation and assessment of services, such outside facilitators must include the council members themselves.

Managers

Since residents come and go, managers are supposed to provide the stabilizing force in public housing. This was not the case with the managers at Rivertown. Improved hiring decisions, as noted above, might help retention. Higher wages and decreases in paperwork and/or office assistants to help with the paperwork might help retention. To increase long-term retention of effective managers, they must be trained in leadership and communication skills so that individuals in the community can trust them.

While a thorough review of factors that impede the long-lasting success of managers is beyond the scope of this book, there is a large literature that HUD could use in hiring and training. As just one example, the following have been identified as important considerations in hiring:

1. Intelligence quotient (how bright one is)
2. Technical/operational quotient (how capable one is of getting things done)
3. Motivational quotient (how driven one is to achieve and grow)
4. Experience quotient (how many requisite skills one possesses)
5. People quotient (how effectively one communicates and works with others)
6. Learning quotient (how deftly one adopts new skills, behaviors and beliefs) (Lominger 2004)

A well-established training program could help compensate for factors that were not sufficient at hiring.

Racial and Class Competency

Managers, community workers, resident council members, and housing authority officials need to be attuned to and understand the racial dynamics of public housing, as well as how those dynamics impact residents' perceptions of the housing authority and affect interaction between residents and housing authority officials. Cultural competency is defined "as a set of congruent behaviors, attitudes, and policies that come together in a system, agency, or among professionals and enables that system, agency, or professionals to work effectively" in cross-cultural situations (Cross et al. 1989; Isaacs and Benjamin 1991; Lee 1997). In other words, knowledge about the group or individuals in question would help produce better outcomes for that agency or system—in this case, the housing authority. As a result of cultural competency training, HUD officials could understand race, ethnicity, and power, factors that have been present throughout the history of public housing, that impact the lack of trust between residents and the housing authority, as well as the impact policies have on residents.

Again, the housing authority could take advantage of outside consultants and facilitators, such as the United Way, the NAACP, the state's civil rights commission, or the Office of Equal Opportunity. Such outside consultants or facilitators could also incorporate the experiences and knowledge of the residents in their training, a process that is vital to bettering the degree to which housing authority officials serve the specialized needs of public housing residents.

RESOURCE DEVELOPMENT

The importance of adequate funding for Rivertown is self-evident. As stated earlier, depending on the political climate and economic stability of the country, HUD is vulnerable to government cuts—but it sometimes also benefits from increases in the budget. Having a limited financial budget from HUD prevents Rivertown and the Ridgeway Public Housing Authority from undertaking certain measures, such as hiring more people to provide services to the residents, increasing the pay of the current employees, and maintaining the buildings. With a stable or decreasing base of funding, the only hope of officials is to secure outside funding. The self-perpetuating nature of the resource problems further impedes action since the lack of funding and time makes writing a grant even less of possibility.

Thus far, Rivertown has not benefited from major government grants. Quebec Gardens, the only public housing community in the city of Ridgeway, received a HOPE VI grant that enabled it to make needed structural changes and maintain its buildings and to provide on-site social service facilities that would assist residents. However, applying for grants takes a lot of time and effort. If each community had its own grant writer, the grant writer could search for and write grant proposals that would meet the specific needs of his or her communities and resident councils. While monies for such a position currently do not exist, building a strong network with other agencies could provide Rivertown and other communities with information about how to hire a grant writer who might also work for social service agencies.

Since money is tight for social service agencies and nonprofits, a collaborative effort must be undertaken between the housing authority and private and public agencies to help secure funding or provide services that would benefit the resident council and council members. Again, hiring additional staff members with a background in fund-raising, networking, and/or grant writing—or even providing sufficient training for current employees—would be extremely beneficial.

At this point, the chapter turns to empowerment suggestions specifically for the seven disjunctions.

EMPHASIS ON CHILDREN

The Rivertown Resident Council clearly articulated a focus on improving the immediate conditions of the community's children. According to the *Code of Federal Regulations*, the housing authority officials, managers, and community workers were supposed to support the council in achieving its focus, but that did not occur. Since the CFR indicates clearly that officials must prioritize the goals of the resident council, assurances must be made that such officials will indeed work toward fulfilling this mandate. However, this is more likely to occur if staff members come to their positions with a solid background or are adequately trained. In order to help the council members better visualize their goals and work toward achieving them—whatever they are—the staff must undergo, as noted above, proper sensitivity and communication training. Moreover, the housing authority officials should be trained to make the resident council aware of the fact that it does have power to "stand up to" officials who do not share its goals. Council members' goals cannot be dismissed—acknowledgment and acceptance of them is, in fact, mandated.

Historically, the Rivertown Resident Council has been undertaking small activities—which is good—but if they had the support of officials, they might be able to do so much more, such as organizing a community day-care center. Of course, the resident council could not create one on its current budget. Thus the earlier discussions are again relative. However, if housing authority officials and others were properly trained or knew how to assist in the pursuit of outside funding, budget woes could be lessened and more monies could be established for the creation of specific goals aimed toward bettering the community. In the meantime, more emphasis could be placed on meeting the community service requirement through a day-care program. Additionally, safety concerns that affect children, such as the grass incident, should receive an immediate response by officials, rather than be embedded in discussions of whose responsibility it is. And managers should be willing to fill in gaps when parents do not assist the resident council. For example, while the managers should be lauded for their financial support of the Kings Island trip, the trip should not have been canceled because of lack parental supervision volunteers. Community workers, interns, or others should have been called upon to assist the council.

LEADERSHIP OF THE COUNCIL

According to the CFR and HUD regulations, resident councils were created to empower public housing residents—to, in effect, give them some autonomy, control, and leadership of their community. According to these regulations, the role of the housing authority officials is to support the council, not manage it or dictate its goals. Just as leadership is learned and takes training, the council members should also be involved in leadership training and workshops. In the workshops, the outside consultants/facilitators would train council members in various methods for empowering themselves and reinforcing the value of their input. Currently, council members do not feel that they are valued or that the authorities listen to their ideas. Such training could help managers learn to be good listeners and support council members. Programs such as Head Start that rely on leadership from parents might provide a model for HUD.

PERCEPTION THAT THE RESIDENT COUNCIL MEMBERS ARE "SNITCHES"

The roles and responsibilities of the housing authority officials and resident council members must be more clearly defined. To begin with, housing authority officials must draft clearer guidelines delineating the parameters of their roles within the council and responsibilities to it. Likewise, council members must draft guidelines outlining their own roles and responsibilities. Such a process could be undertaken more effectively by an outside consultant with no ties to either group—someone who can objectively assess the two groups and offer guidelines based upon those interpretations.

Also, measures must be undertaken to dispel the conception that council members are "snitches" who report directly to the housing authority. Care must be taken to articulate clearly and strongly to all residents an awareness of the fact that the council is a self-governing body whose sole responsibility is bettering the life of the community as a whole—not reporting lease violations, problems, or the sorts of activities best left to management. Only when all members of the community are made aware of this fact will trust build between all involved parties.

RESPONSIBILITIES OF THE RESIDENT COUNCIL AND HUD OFFICIALS AND MANAGER/MANAGERIAL STYLES

Again, no clearly defined roles and responsibilities exist for the resident council, HUD officials, and managers. When individuals work for the housing authority, they are simply thrown into the mix. I return to the grass incident as an example. This is unacceptable. A central factor in the role confusion among housing officials is that no one seemed to know what his or her role was to the council. By establishing clear guidelines, having a training manual, and making sure managers and housing officials are property trained, housing authority officials could ensure that each individual knew his or her role and responsibilities—and maintained them appropriately. Working in social services is a demanding and at times daunting task, so providing housing authority officials with peer mentors might also prove a worthwhile endeavor. The same is true for managers. In addition to getting feedback from the housing authority and residents, managers could work with their own private peer mentors. Whatever effort is undertaken, it must work toward ensuring a balanced relationship between managers, housing authority officials, and council members.

MEETING DYNAMICS

According to this research, resident council members feel that they are required to attend far too many meetings beyond their regular council sessions. Serving on the resident council is voluntary; HUD should consider changing its regulations to make participation a paid position given the huge demands on their time. Even if the council stays a voluntary organization and HUD expects residents to become more involved, then it might consider paying them, at least paying them more than they currently are receiving. The financial remunerations were partly because of the amount of work that was expected. This could have contributed as well to the lack of participation in the council. Alternatively, they could provide them with extra services as compensation for their time.

As it stands now, the CFR requires residents to attend a certain number of meetings, which council members believe did not work in their best interest. HUD could simply stop this requirement and allow residents to attend when they feel they have issues worth discussing.

While the current structure of the meetings of the resident council played important roles in developing social support, council members could still benefit from an understanding of more traditional techniques for running a meeting. If the council became aware that its elected leader was in charge of meetings, domination by the managers and others would be less likely to occur. Once again, an outside consultation/facilitator or new hire (with specialized skills) could help train council members on developing effective meeting techniques. Housing officials would have to be more aware of their supportive role at meetings as well.

HUD STRUCTURE AND PRIORITIES

To establish a stronger and more trusting relationship with council members, HUD officials should perhaps reconsider certain laws and policies that many residents and their representatives on the council currently consider "hypocritical." A few of these have been noted above. Rather than a "top-down" approach, a "bottom-up" approach might serve as a more logical paradigm considering the helplessness and lack of trust that has often characterized the lives of public housing residents. However, one danger with the "bottom-up" approach is the fact that council members—traditionally hesitant about exerting themselves—might tend to feel that, in truth, they and their efforts are subordinate to the interests, interpretations, and assumptions of the managers, housing authority officials, and community workers—in short, subordinate to everyone.

Again I mention the community service requirement. The community service requirement, which requires residents to volunteer eight hours a month to live in public housing, was created to encourage residents to become more self-sufficient and join the resident council. However, HUD officials did not consider the fact that managers are routinely overworked and that this requirement would simply increase their workload without really resulting in any benefits for the community as a whole. The lack of time for housing officials to help the resident council was a theme during the interviews. Deleting this one requirement would certainly help. If the CSR is not going to be eliminated, which is my main suggestion, then at a minimum, use it more effectively.

The situation of a housing development like Rivertown is not helped by HUD policies that tend to prioritize severely distressed public housing complexes or to highlight the stellar examples of positive, self-sufficient public housing communities. Rivertown is neither of these, but is in fact what one might call "middle line." Little attention, monies, or policies focus on middle-line upkeep. I recall the overflowing trash bins that I saw upon my early visit as an example of one type of neglect. To be sure, Rivertown is all right—for now. It's not severely distressed nor is it a stellar example of public housing. However, if support and upkeep are not given, it could eventually fall into the two former category.

Moreover, when it comes to HUD policies regarding resident councils, some inconsistency exists between the ideal and the real. Although HUD policies and laws express explicit support for resident councils, the lack of enforcement, monitoring, and training of HUD field officials often ensures that such policies are not maintained as they should be. As a result, the resident councils so heralded by HUD as providing a voice for the community often fall victim to the very policies that created them.

If an agency is truly dedicated to empowering residents and resident councils and giving them voice, it must realize that time, money, and energy must be spent toward helping these groups achieve their goals. Moreover, a truly concerned agency must develop a new way of thinking about policies, management, and the very residents of public housing itself. Such endeavors are not left to HUD alone, though. In fact, success depends on massive effort and dedication from HUD, housing authority officials, managers, community workers, and the members of the resident council alike.

If "bottom-up" policies are to work in public housing, then the assumptions that HUD officials hold about the residents need to be altered dramatically: they must come to understand how lived experiences must be a part of any planning designed to impact community building through the work of the resident council.

NOTES

1. Intersectional analysis now stands at the forefront of contemporary theory and practice in feminist cultural studies, critical race studies, racial/ethnic studies, and multiculturalism. As Dill, Nettles, and Weber (2001, 4) point out, the systematic study of intersectionality is "flexible enough to consider large-scale, historically constructed and hierarchical power systems and the politics of personal interactions, including meanings and representations in the experience of individuals."

Legal theorist Kimberlé Crenshaw, in "Mapping the Margins: Intersectionality, Identity Politics, and Violence against Women of Color" (1995a), distinguishes structural intersectionality, in which the location of women of color at the intersection of race and gender make experiences of rape, domestic violence, and remedial reform qualitatively different from that of white women, and political intersectionality, in which antisexist and antiracist rhetoric operate in tandem to marginalize the issue of violence against women. Philomena Essed, in *Understanding Everyday Racism* (1991), develops intersectionality as a tool to identify intertwined gender, race, ethnic, gender, economic, and educational factors in shaping specific expressions of everyday injustices. Intersectional analysis, and particularly Crenshaw's and Essed's work, has become influential as a policy framework in the arena of international women's rights. For example, various bodies and entities within the United Nations have to a certain extent recognized the intersectionality of discrimination in women's lives, that women do not experience discrimination and other forms of human rights violations solely on the grounds of gender, but also age, disability, health status, race, ethnicity, caste, class, national origin, and sexual orientation. See Working Group on Women and Human Rights, "Background Briefing on Intersectionality," http://www.crge.umd.edu/.

2. Leadership development and leadership development training teaches individuals how to recognize what is and is not working in their organization and how to improve it by acquiring effective leadership skills—whether through communication, self-awareness, social awareness, or self-management. Mussig (2003) states that leadership is built on values, trust, and credibility—factors that are reflective of the relationship as a behavior. Also see the American Society for Training and Development (ASTD) on leadership. For example, Karlin Sloan & Company, one of many leadership development consultant firms, offers leadership training in the following areas: communication, decision making, delegation, continuous improvement, diversity awareness, listening, teamwork, managing meetings, thinking styles, and influence.

3. That is, housing authority, community workers, and managers.

4. That is, housing authority, community workers, and managers.

Appendix A

Table 7.1.   Legal Cases from Resident Councils/ Community Groups against the Housing Authority and HUD

Issue	Case
Homes/Community Being Threatened	Little Earth of United Tribes, Inc. v. United States Dep't of Housing & Urban Dev., Civ. No. 3-82-1096, UNITED STATES DISTRICT COURT FOR THE DISTRICT OF MINNESOTA, THIRD DIVISION, 584 F. Supp. 1301; 1983 U.S. Dist. LEXIS 14470, August 19, 1983. Retrieved on March 2, 2003, from http://web.lexis-nexis.com
	Cabrini-Green Advisory Council v. Chicago Hous. Auth., No. 96 c 6949, UNITED STATES DISTRICT COURT FOR THE NORTHERN DISTRICT OF ILLINOIS, EASTERN DIVISION, 1997 U.S. Dist. LEXIS 625, January 21, 1997, Decided, January 22, 1997, DOCKETED. Retrieved on March 2, 2003, from http://web.lexis-nexis.com
	Resident Council of Allen Parkway Village v. United States Dep't of Hous. & Urban Dev., No. 91-2454., UNITED STATES COURT OF APPEALS FOR THE FIFTH CIRCUIT, 980 F.2d 1043; 1993 U.S. App. LEXIS 330; 24 Fed. R. Serv. 3d (Callaghan) 1100, January 13, 1993, Decided, As Corrected. Rehearing Denied February 26, 1993, Reported at 1993 U.S. App. LEXIS 4579. Retrieved on March 2, 2003, from http://web.lexis-nexis.com
	Alexandria Resident Council, Inc. v. Alexandria Redevelopment & Hous. Auth., No. 00-2538, UNITED STATES COURT OF APPEALS FOR THE FOURTH CIRCUIT, 11 Fed. Appx. 283; 2001 U.S. App. LEXIS 11865, May 7, 2001, Argued, June 6, 2001, Decided, RULES OF THE FOURTH CIRCUIT COURT OF APPEALS MAY LIMIT CITATION TO UNPUBLISHED OPINIONS. PLEASE

REFER TO THE RULES OF THE UNITED STATES
COURT OF APPEALS FOR THIS CIRCUIT. Retrieved on
March 2, 2003, from http://web.lexis-nexis.com

Alexandria Resident Council v. Samuel Madden Homes
Tenant Council, No. 97-2501, No. 97-2502, UNITED
STATES COURT OF APPEALS FOR THE FOURTH
CIRCUIT, 1998 U.S. App. LEXIS 16749, June 3, 1998,
Argued, July 22, 1998, Decided, RULES OF THE FOURTH
CIRCUIT COURT OF APPEALS MAY LIMIT CITATION TO
UNPUBLISHED OPINIONS. PLEASE REFER TO THE
RULES OF THE UNITED STATES COURT OF APPEALS
FOR THIS CIRCUIT., Reported in Table Case Format at:
1998 U.S. App. LEXIS 26356. Certiorari Denied January 19,
1999, Reported at: 1999 U.S. LEXIS 624. Retrieved on
March 2, 2003, from http://web.lexis-nexis.com

Bosely v. Euclid, No. 73-1608, UNITED STATES COURT
OF APPEALS FOR THE SIXTH CIRCUIT, 496 F.2d 193;
1974 U.S. App. LEXIS 8825, May 3, 1974, Decided.
Retrieved on March 2, 2003, from http://web.lexis-
nexis.com

Jones v. Housing Auth., CIVIL ACTION NO. 93-0717-BH-C,
UNITED STATES DISTRICT COURT FOR THE
SOUTHERN DISTRICT OF ALABAMA, SOUTHERN
DIVISION, 1995 U.S. Dist. LEXIS 13384, August 9, 1995,
Decided, August 9, 1995, FILED Retrieved on March 2,
2003, from http://web.lexis-nexis.com

Winter v. D.C. HUD Field Office, Civil Action No.: 00-2706
(RMU), Doc. Nos.: 3, 4, 6, UNITED STATES DISTRICT
COURT FOR THE DISTRICT OF COLUMBIA, 150 F. Supp.
2d 27; 2001 U.S. Dist. LEXIS 14881, April 2, 2001, Decided.
Retrieved on March 2, 2003, from http://web.lexis-
nexis.com

Concerned Residents of Taylor-Wythe v. New York City
Hous. Auth., 96 Civ. 2349 (RWS), UNITED STATES
DISTRICT COURT FOR THE SOUTHERN DISTRICT OF
NEW YORK, 1996 U.S. Dist. LEXIS 11460, August 8, 1996,
Decided, August 9, 1996, FILED Retrieved on March 2,
2003, from http://web.lexis-nexis.com

Informal Organizations
Not Recognized

MUNGIOVI v. CHICAGO HOUS. AUTH., Case No. 94 C
6663, UNITED STATES DISTRICT COURT FOR THE
NORTHERN DISTRICT OF ILLINOIS, EASTERN
DIVISION, 914 F. Supp. 207; 1995 U.S. Dist. LEXIS 14008,
September 20, 1995, Decided, September 22, 1995,
DOCKETED. Retrieved on March 2, 2003, from http://
web.lexis-nexis.com

Alazan-Apache Resident Ass'n v. San Antonio Hous. Auth.,
CIVIL NO. SA-94-CA-0106, UNITED STATES DISTRICT
COURT FOR THE WESTERN DISTRICT OF TEXAS, SAN

ANTONIO DIVISION, 885 F. Supp. 949; 1995 U.S. Dist. LEXIS 22288, January 31, 1995, Decided, January 31, 1995, Filed. Retrieved on March 2, 2003, from http:// web.lexis-nexis.com

St. Bernard Resident Council ex rel. Leblanc v. Mason, CIVIL ACTION NO. 96-1698 SECTION "T"(4), UNITED STATES DISTRICT COURT FOR THE EASTERN DISTRICT OF LOUISIANA, 1997 U.S. Dist. LEXIS 12036, August 6, 1997, Decided, August 6, 1997, Filed; August 8, 1997, Entered. Retrieved on March 2, 2003, from http:// web.lexis-nexis.com

Appendix B

LAYOUT OF RIVERTOWN

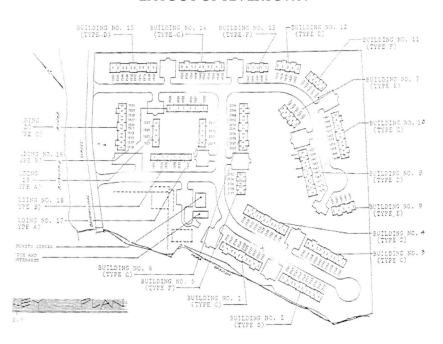

RIVERTOWN FLYERS—RECRUITMENT

YOU CAN MAKE A DIFFERENCE

- *Do you want to do something positive with your time?*

- *Do you want to have control over decisions that are being made in* Rivertown

- *Do you want to make a difference in your Community?*

- *Do you want to improve the current Council?*

IF you answered yes to any of these questions and are interested in Joining the Rivertown *Resident council*
Please call: 427-1288 or see one of the Council Reps.

RIVERTOWN FLYERS—NEWS AND SITE-BASED MEETING

| Rivertown | RESIDENT NEWS 4/04 |

CLEAN VALLEY DAY IS SCHEDULED FOR SATURDAY, APRIL 5. WE WILL BE GATHERING IN THE COMMUNITY ROOM AT 9:00 A.M. RAIN OR SHINE.

We would like for all residents to participate by cleaning the area where they live such as the front and back yards, washing down the front and back screen doors, cleaning the curb in front of their buildings or around the dumpster.

I would like to thank all of you for the great work you did on the HUD annual inspections.

Just a reminder: Please do not sit out in public and drink alcoholic beverages or smoke controlled substances. Residents who participate in this activity will be sent a lease violation. You are responsible for your guest at all times and the activities that occur at your home.

It will be expected that you keep your yards clean and free of all items that are an eyesore. Please refer to your lease.

You are not allowed to make any alterations to the property. This includes fencing of any type, structures built onto the porches such as wood or lattice, chaining items to gas poles or clotheslines. Do not store any gas-powered items other than a lawnmower outside. Do not leave your clothing on the line longer than 8 hours.

LOUD MUSIC and LOUD NOISE that disturbs your neighbor could result in the police being called to settle the situation. Please respect your neighbors' right to the peaceful enjoyment of their home.

UNAUTHORIZED GUESTS WILL CAUSE YOU TO LOSE YOUR APARTMENT. PLEASE REFER TO YOUR LEASE.

Please do not allow your children to cut through the creek alone. There have been reports of crime occurring in the location.

A COPY OF THIS FLYER WILL BE PUT IN ALL OF THE RESIDENT FILES.

Rivertown PLACE SITE BASE MEETING AGENDA
October 9, 2002 AT 10:30 A.M.

Time: 10:30 a.m. in the Resident Council Office Area

Facilitator: Vanessa Property Manager

To: See Distribution List

AGENDA

- Welcome
- Introduction of New Resident Council Members
- Discussion of application process
- Activities update
- Housing Authority changes/updates

Thanking each of you in advance for your attendance

Cc: **Daniel Harrison**

RIVERTOWN FLYER — NOTICE

Partners in Progress

**IMPORTANT NOTICE
TO ALL RESIDENTS
MAY 10, 2002**

ON MAY 1, 2002, THE COURT PROCESSING FEE FOR UNLAWFUL DETAINERS WAS INCREASED FROM $18.00 TO $22.00. PLEASE BE ADVISED THAT BEGINNING MAY 2002 IF YOU RECEIVE AN UNLAWFUL DETAINER YOU WILL BE CHARGED $22.00. TO AVOID BEING CHARGED THIS FEE PLEASE PAY YOUR RENT IN FULL BY MAY 25, 2002.

Rivertown   **RESIDENT NEWS**

Job Prep, a program designed to help you with job interview skills will have 3 sessions starting May 7, 2002. Transportation and childcare will be provided. Please see Ms. Evans for the applications.

The   City Police Department will host a "Bike Rodeo" on June 8, 2002.

Even Start will have a clothing fair on Monday, April 22 in the community room.

Church of the Harvest will have a women's ministry program on Saturday, April 20 in the community room.

Apple Ridge Farm will have health screenings for summer camp on Thursday May 23, 2002 in the community room 4:30 to 7:00 p.m.

NEW POSTAL CHANGES ON SITE EFFECTIVE MAY 2002. THE POSTMAN WILL NOT LEAVE ANY MAIL TO PERSONS NOT ON THE LEASE.

THE POSTMAN WILL PUT IN ALL NAME CHANGES. PLEASE DO NOT TAMPER WITH THE PLASTIC NAME STICKER INSIDE THE BOX. MAIL WILL NOT BE DELIVERED TO ANY MAILBOX THAT HAS BEEN TAMPERED WITH BY A TENANT.

Children are not allowed to play on the rental office parking lot or enter the office premises unsupervised.

**HOUSING
AUTHORITY**

Partners in Progress

Dear Residents:

For the health and safety of all residents, and in an effort to maintain the housing developments in a safe and sanitary condition, the City of _____ and Housing Authority has put into effect a Housekeeping Policy.

The policy is directed to those residents who are in violation of their lease as the result of unsatisfactory housekeeping conditions which create fire and health hazards. Section 8 of your lease states:

"Resident agrees to…keep the premises free from all trash, ashes, garbage, rubbish and other debris by disposing of it in a sanitary and safe manner. Resident agrees to conduct himself…in a manner which will be…conducive to maintaining the Development in a safe and sanitary condition."

If unsatisfactory housekeeping conditions are reported to the Housing Authority, the Manager will inspect the apartment and discuss the problem with the resident. If the problem is not resolved, the resident will be given written notice of the violations, which must be corrected within 21 days. A second inspection will then be made. If the violations have not been corrected, a 30-day moving notice will be issued.

If the violations are corrected but similar violations reoccur within six (6) months, the resident will receive a 30-day moving notice. The resident will not be given another 21-day grace period during which to correct the re-occurring violaitons.

If you have any questions concerning this policy, please discuss them with your Manager.

I have read and understand
The above policy.   Sincerely,

                                                                               , PHM

_____
Signature

_____
Date

May 2003

Monday	Tuesday	Wednesday	Thursday	Friday	Sat/Sun
April 28	29	30	May 1	2	3
8:30am CASA Training starts	9:00am REEXAMS-AUGUST	5:00pm Girl Scouts (Resource Center)		SCHEDULE INTERVIEW APPTS (9:00am add calendar items 10:30am Resident Council Meeting (community 3:00pm Employee meeting at Melrose Towers 4:00pm Boy Scouts	4
5	6	7	8	9	10
	2:00pm Staff Meeting/COPE (Melrose Towers)	5:00pm Girl Scouts (Resource Center)		SCHEDULE INTERVIEW APPTS (10:30am Resident Council Meeting (community 3:00pm Quarterly Employee Meeting 4:00pm Boy Scouts (Community Room)	11
12	13	14	15	16	17
1:00pm Vickie Dalton/Rke City Schools (Community Room)		9:00am APPLE RIDGE HEALTH SCREENING 9:00am RENT CREDITS DUE ON 15 EACH MONTH 10:30am Site Base Meeting (Jamestown) 5:00pm Girl Scouts (Resource		SCHEDULE INTERVIEW APPTS (10:30am Resident Council Meeting (community room) 4:00pm Boy Scouts (Community Room)	18
19	20	21	22	23	24
	3:00pm staff Meeting (Melrose Towers)	5:00pm Girl Scouts (Resource Center)		SCHEDULE INTERVIEW APPTS (10:30am Resident Council Meeting (community room) 4:00pm Boy Scouts (Community Room)	25
26	27	28	29	30	31
		5:00pm Girl Scouts (Resource Center)		SCHEDULE INTERVIEW APPTS (10:30am Resident Council Meeting (community room) 4:00pm Boy Scouts (Community Room)	June 1

Bibliography

Albelda, Randy, Nancy Folbre, and the Center for Popular Economics. 1996. *The War on the Poor: A Defense Manual*. New York: New York Press.

Ambert, Anne-Marie, Patricia A. Alder, Peter Alder, and Daniel F. Detzner. 1995. "Understanding and Evaluating Qualitative Research." *Journal of Marriage and the Family* 57 (4): 879–93.

Amott, Teresa, and Julie Matthaei. 1996. *Race, Gender, and Work*. New York: South End.

Anderson, Elijah. 1990. *Streetwise: Race, Class, and Change in an Urban Community*. Chicago: University of Chicago Press.

Andrews, Kenneth T. 2001. "Social Movements and Policy Implementation: The Mississippi Civil Rights Movement and the War on Poverty, 1965–1971." *American Sociological Review* 66:71–95.

Arp, William, III, and Keith A. Boeckelman. 1994. "Emerging Black Environmentalism: A Consequence of Pollution and Its Threat to Health." *Southeastern Political Review* 22:775–86.

Ashbaugh, Sam. 2001. "The Government Performance and Results Act: Lessons for State and Local Governments." *Government Finance Review*, April 19–21.

"Association for Talent Development". Retrieved January 2013. https://www.td.org/.

Avolio, Bruce J., and Bernard Bass. 1995. "Individual Consideration Viewed at Multiple Levels of Analysis: A Multi-Level Framework for Examining the Diffusion of Transformational Leadership." *Leadership Quarterly* 66 (2): 199–219.

Bailey, Carol A. 1996. *A Guide to Field Research*. Thousand Oaks, Calif.: Pine Forge.

Barot, Rohit, and John Bird. 2001. "Racialization: The Genealogy and Critique of a Concept." *Ethnic and Racial Studies* 24 (4): 601–18.

Becker, Howard S. 1963. *Outsiders*. New York: Free Press.

Bell, Derrick. 1995. "Racial Realism." In *Critical Race Theory: The Key Writings That Formed the Movement*, edited by Kimberlé Crenshaw, Neil Gotanda, Gary Peller, and Kendall Thomas, 302–14. New York: New Press.

———. 2000. *Race, Racism and American Law*. 4th ed. Aspen, Colo.: Aspen Pub..

Bellah, Robert N., Richard Madsen, William M. Sullivan, Ann Swidler, and Steven M. Tipton. 1985. *Habits of the Heart: Individualism and Commitment in American Life*. Berkeley: University of California Press.

Belle, Deborah, and Joanne Doucet. 2003. "Poverty, Inequality, and Discrimination as Sources of Depression among U.S. Women." *Psychology of Women Quarterly* 27:101–13.

Bender, Thomas. 1992. *Community and Social Change in America*. Baltimore: Rutgers University Press.

Berg, Bruce L. 2001. *Qualitative Research Methods for the Social Sciences.* Boston: Allyn & Bacon.

Bergerson, Amy Aldous. 2003. "Critical Race Theory and White Racism: Is There Room for White Scholars in Fighting Racism in Education?" *Qualitative Studies in Education* 16 (1): 51–63.

Bernal, Dolores Delgado. 2002. "Critical Race Theory, Latino Critical Theory, and Critical Raced-Gendered Epistemologies: Recognizing Students of Colors as Holders and Creators of Knowledge." *Qualitative Inquiry* 8 (1): 105–26.

Bickford, Adam, and Douglas S. Massey. 1991. "Segregation in the Second Ghetto: Racial and Ethnic Segregation in American Public Housing, 1977." *Social Forces* 69 (4): 1011–36.

Bolland, John M. 2001. "In Search of a Few Hundred Good Kids: Three Months in the Life of a Community-Based Survey Research Study." *Families in Society: The Journal of Contemporary Human Services* 82 (1).

Bolland, John M., and Debra Moehle McCallum. 2002. "Neighboring and Community Mobilization in High Poverty City Neighborhoods." *Urban Affairs Review* 38 (1): 42–69.

Bonilla-Silva, Eduardo. 2003. *Racism without Racists: Colorblind Racism and the Persistence of Racial Inequality in the United States.* New York: Rowman & Littlefield.

Bourdieu, Pierre. 1986. "The Forms of Capital." In *Handbook of Theory and Research for the Sociology of Education,* edited by J. G. Richardson, 241–58. New York: Greenwood.

Bowie, Stan. 2001. "The Impact of Privatized Management in Urban Public Housing Communities: A Comparative Analysis of Perceived Crime, Neighborhood Problems, and Personal Safety." *Journal of Sociology and Social Welfare* 28 (4): 67–81.

Brager, George, Harry Specht, and James L. Torezyner. 1987. *Community Organizing.* New York: Columbia University Press.

Brooks, Margaret. 2004. "Drawing the Social Construction of Knowledge." *Australian Journal of Early Childhood* 29 (4): 577–84.

Brown, Dorothy A. 2003. *Critical Race Theory: Cases, Materials, and Problems.* St. Paul, Minn.: West.

Browne, Irene, Cynthia Hewitt, Leann Tigges, and Gary Green. 2001. "Why Does Job Segregation Lead to Wage Inequality among African-Americans? Person, Place, Sector, or Skills." *Social Science Research* 30:473–95.

Browne-Ferrigno, Tricia, and Rodney Muth. 2004. "Leadership Mentoring in Clinical Practice: Role Socialization, Professional Development and Capacity Building." *Educational Administration Quarterly* 40 (4): 468–94.

Brunson, Liesette, Frances E. Kuo, and William C. Sullivan. 2001. "Resident Appropriation of Defensible Space in Public Housing: Implications for Safety and Community." *Environment and Behavior* 33 (5): 626–52.

Bryman, Alan, Mike Stephens, and Charlotte Campo. 1996. "The Importance of Context: Qualitative Research and the Study of Leadership." *Leadership Quarterly* 7 (3): 353–70.

Bullard, Robert D. 1992. *Race and the Incidence of Environmental Hazards: A Time for Discourse.* Boulder, Colo.: Westview.

Bullard, Robert D., J. Eugene Grigsby, and Charles Lee, eds. 1994. *Residential Apartheid: The American Legacy.* Los Angeles: University of California Center for Afro American Studies.

Bullock, Heather E., and Wendy M. Limbert. 2003. "Scaling the Socioeconomic Ladder: Low-Income Women's Perceptions of Class Status and Opportunity." *Journal of Social Issues* 59 (4): 693–709.

Bunting, Sheila M. 1996. "Sources of Stigma Associated with Women with HIV." *Advances in Nursing Science* 19 (2): 64–74.

Care, James H. 1998. "The Complexity of Segregation: Why It Continues." *Vital Speeches* 64 (20): 627–31.

Carlile, Jennifer. 1990. "Public Housing—Home Sweet Home? In an Attempt to Rescue Their Homes from Drug Dealers and Gangs, Many Public Housing Residents Are Turning to Tenant Management." *American City and Country* 105 (7): 64–68.

Carr, James H., and Isaac F. Megbolugbe. 1993. "The Federal Reserve Bank of Boston Study on Mortgage Lending Revisited." *Journal of Housing Research* 4 (2): 277–313.

Carter, William H., Michael H. Schill, and Susan M. Wachter. 1998. "Polarisation, Public Housing and Racial Minorities in U.S. Cities." *Urban Studies* 35 (10): 1889.

Ceballo, Rosario, and Vonnie C. McLoyd. 2002. "Social Support and Parenting in Poor, Dangerous Neighborhoods." *Child Development* 73 (4): 1310–21.

CFR (*Code of Federal Regulations*). 2004. Title 24, Volume 4, Parts 700 to 1699. Revised as of April 1, 1997, pp. 650–65. From the U.S. Government Publishing Office via GPO Access.

Chaskin, Robert J. 2001. "Building Community Capacity: A Definitional Framework and Case Studies from a Comprehensive Community Initiative." *Urban Affairs Review* 36 (3): 291–324.

Christensen, Donna H., Carla M. Dahl, and Kathryn D. Rettig. 1990. "Noncustodial Mothers and Child Support: Examining the Larger Context." *Family Relations* 39:388–94.

Christenson, James A., and Jerry W. Robinson. 1980. *Community Development in America.* Ames: Iowa State University Press.

Clawson, Rosalee A. 2002. "Poor People, Black Faces: The Portrayal of Poverty in Economics Textbooks." *Journal of Black Studies* 32 (3): 352–62.

Clawson, Rosalee A., and Rakuya Trice. 2000. "Poverty and We Know It: Media Portrayals of the Poor." *Public Opinion Quarterly* 64 (1): 53–64.

Coates, Rodney D. 2003. "Law and the Cultural Production of Race and Racialized Systems of Oppression: Early American Court Cases." *American Behavioral Scientist* 47 (3): 329–32.

Cole, Elizabeth R., and Safiya R. Omari. 2003. "Race, Class and the Dilemmas of Upward Mobility for African Americans." *Journal of Social Issues* 59 (4): 785–803.

Coleman, James. 1988. "Social Capital in the Creation of Human Capital." *American Journal of Sociology* 94:S95–S120.

Coley, Rebekah L., Frances E. Kuo, and William Sullivan. 1997. "Where Does Community Grow? The Context Created by Nature in Urban Public Housing." *Environment and Behavior* 29 (4): 468–95.

Collins, Patricia Hill. 2000. *Black Feminist Thought: Knowledge, Consciousness, and the Politics of Empowerment.* New York: Routledge.

Condit, Celeste M., and John Louis Lucaites. 1993. *Crafting Equality: America's Anglo-African Word.* Chicago: University of Chicago Press.

Conley, Dalton. 2001. "The Black-White Wealth Gap: Net Worth, More Than Any Other Statistics, Shows the Depth of Racial Inequality." *Nation* magazine, March 26.

"Consortium on Race, Gender, and Ethnicity." University of Maryland. Retrieved January 2013. http://www.crge.umd.edu

Conyers, James E. 2002. "Racial Inequality: Emphasis on Explanations." *Western Journal of Black Studies* 26 (4): 249–54.

Copeland, Valire Carr, and Kimberly Snyder. 2011. "Barriers to Mental Health Treatment Services for Low Income African American Women Whose Children Receive Behavioral Service: An Ethnographic Investigation." *Social Work in Public Health* 26: 78–95.

Cose, Ellis. 1993. *The Rage of a Privileged Class.* New York: HarperCollins.

Crain, Marion. 2002. "Critical Race Studies: Colorblind Unionism." *UCLA Law Review* 49:1313.

Crenshaw, Kimberlé. 1995a. "Mapping the Margins: Intersectionality, Identity Politics, and Violence against Women of Color." In *Critical Race Theory: The Key Writings That Formed the Movement*, edited by Kimberlé Crenshaw, Neil Gotanda, Gary Peller, and Kendall Thomas, 357–83. New York: New Press.

———. 1995b. "Race, Reform, and Retrenchment: Transformation and Legitimation in Anti-Discrimination Law." In *Critical Race Theory: The Key Writings That Formed the Movement*, edited by Kimberlé Crenshaw, Neil Gotanda, Gary Peller, and Kendall Thomas, 103–26. New York: New Press.

———. 2002. "The First Decade: Critical Reflections, or a Foot in the Closing Door." In *Crossroads, Directions, and a New Critical Race Theory*, edited by Francisco Valdes, Merome McCristal Culp, and Angela P. Harris, 9–31. Philadelphia: Temple University Press.

Crenshaw, Kimberlé, Neil Gotanda, Gary Peller, and Kendall Thomas, eds. 1995. *Critical Race Theory: The Key Writings That Formed the Movement.* New York: New Press.

Creswell, John. W. 1998. *Qualitative Inquiry and Research Design: Choosing among Five Traditions*. Thousand Oaks, Calif.: Sage.

Cross, Terry L., Barbara J. Bazron, Karl W. Dennis, and Mareasa R. Isaacs. 1989. *Towards a Culturally Competent System of Care: Volume I*. Washington, D.C.: CASSP Technical Assistance Center, Georgetown University Child Development Center.

Crump, Jeff R. 2003. "The End of Public Housing as We Know It: Public Housing Policy, Labor Regulation and the US City." *International Journal of Urban and Regional Research* 27 (1):179–87.

Currie, Janet, and Aaron Yelowitz. 2000. "Are Public Housing Projects Good for Kids?" *Journal of Public Economics* 75 (1): 99–124.

Danziger, Sheldon, and Ann Chih Lin. 2000. "Coping with Poverty: The Social Contexts of Neighborhood, Work and Family in the African-American Community." *Perspectives: African American Research* 6:41–51.

Darden, Joe T. 1994. "African American Residential Segregation: An Examination of Race and Class in Metropolitan Detroit." In *Residential Apartheid: The American Legacy*, edited by Robert D. Bullard, J. Eugene Grigsby, and Charles Lee, 82–95. Los Angeles: University of California Center for Afro American Studies.

Dawson, Michael C. 1994. *Behind the Mule: Race and Class in African-American Policies*. Princeton, N.J.: Princeton University Press.

———. 2000. "Slowly Coming to Grips with the Effects of the American Racial Order on American Policy Preferences." In *Racialized Politics: The Debate about Racism in America*, edited by David O. Sears, Jim Sidanius, and Lawrence Bobo, 344–58. Chicago: University of Chicago Press.

Delgado, Richard. 1989. "Symposium, Legal Storytelling." *Michigan Law Review* 87:2073.

———. 1990. "When a Story Is Just a Story: Does Voice Really Matter?" *Virginia Law Review* 76:95–111.

Delgado, Richard, and Jean Stefancic. 1995. "The Social Construction of Brown v. Board of Education: Law Reform and the Reconstructive Paradox." *William and Mary Law Review* 36 (2): 547–70.

———, ed. 1997. *Critical White Studies: Looking Behind The Mirror*. Philadelphia: Temple University Press.

Denzin, Norman K., and Yvonna S. Lincoln, eds. 1994. *Handbook of Qualitative Research*. Thousand Oaks, Calif.: Sage.

———, eds. 2000. *Handbook of Qualitative Research*. 2nd ed. Thousand Oaks, Calif.: Sage.

Dill, B.T., S. M. Nettles, and L. Weber. "What Do We Mean by Intersections?" Spring 2001. Connections: Newsletter of Consortium for Research on Race, Gender, and Ethnicity 4.

Domhoff, G. William. 2002. *Who Rules America? Power and Politics*. New York: McGraw-Hill.

Dreier, Peter, John Mollenkopf, and Todd Swanstrom. 2001. *Place Matters: Metropolitics for the Twenty-First Century*. Lawrence: University Press of Kansas.

Du Bois, W. E. B. 1978. *On Sociology and the Black Community*. Edited by Dan S. Green and Edwin D. Driver. Chicago: University of Chicago Press.

Dymski, Gary A. 1995. "The Theory of Bank Rekindling and Discrimination: An Exploration." *Review of Black Political Economy* 23 (Winter): 37–75.

Dymski, Gary A., and John M. Veitch. 1994. "Taking It to the Bank: Race, Credit, and Income in Los Angeles." In *Residential Apartheid: The American Legacy*, edited by Robert D. Bullard, J. Eugene Grigsby, and Charles Lee, 150–80. Los Angeles: University of California Center for Afro American Studies.

Edin, Kathryn, and Laura Lein. 1997. *Making Ends Meet: How Single Mothers Survive Welfare and Low Wage Work*. New York: Sage.

Edwards, Korie. L. 2014. "Role Strain Theory and Understanding the Role of Head Cleary of Racially Diverse Churches." *Sociology of Religion* 75 (1): 57–79.

Effrat, Marcia Pelly, ed. 1974. *The Community: Approaches and Applications*. New York: Free Press.

Emerson, Richard M. 1962. "Power Dependence Relations." *American Sociological Review* 27 (1): 31–41.

Espiritu, Ye Le. 1997. *Asian American Women and Men: Labor, Laws, and Love.* Thousand Oaks, CA: Sage.

Essed, Philomena. 1991. *Understanding Everyday Racism: An Interdisciplinary Theory.* Thousand Oaks, CA: Sage.

Etzioni, Amitai. 1993. *The Spirit of Community: Rights, Responsibilities, and the Communitarian Agenda.* New York: Crown.

Faircloth, Christopher A. 2001. "'Those People' and Troubles Talk Social Typing and Community Construction in Senior Public Housing." *Journal of Aging Studies* 15 (4): 333–51.

Fantasia, Rick. 1988. *Cultures of Solidarity.* Los Angeles: University of California Press.

Farley, Reynolds, Elaine L. Fielding, and Maria Krysan. 1997. "The Residential Preferences of Blacks and Whites: A Four Metropolis Analysis." *Housing Policy Debate* 8 (4): 763–800.

Feagin, Joe. 1991. "The Continuing Significance of Race: Antiblack Discrimination in Public Places." *American Sociological Review* 56 (1): 101–17.

———. 1994. "A House Is Not a Home: White Racism and US Housing Practices." In *Residential Apartheid: The American Legacy,* edited by Robert D. Bullard, J. Eugene Grigsby, and Charles Lee, 17–48. Los Angeles: University of California Center for Afro American Studies.

———. 2000. *Racist America: Roots, Current Realities, and Future Reparations.* New York: Routledge.

Feagin, Joe, Hernan Vera, and Pinar Batur. 2001. *White Racism.* New York: Routledge.

Ferguson, Ronald F., and William T. Dickens, eds. 1999. *Urban Problems and Community Development.* Washington, D.C.: Brookings Institution.

Finkel, Andrew E., Karin A. Lennon, and Elizabeth R. Eisenstadt. 2000. "Hope VI: A Promising Vintage?" *Review of Policy Research* 17 (2/3): 104–18.

Fischer, Mary J., and Douglas S. Massey. 2000. "Residential Segregation and Ethnic Enterprise in US Metropolitan Areas." *Social Problems* 47 (3): 408.

Fitzgerald, John M., and Christopher Riber. 2004. "Welfare Reform and Female Headship." *Demography* 41 (2): 189–212.

Flippen, Chenoa A. 2001. "Racial and Ethnic Inequality in Homeownership and Housing Equity." *Sociological Quarterly* 44 (2): 121–40.

Foster-Fishman, Pennie G., Deborah A. Salem, Susan Chibnall, Ray Legler, and Courtney Yapchai. 1998. "Empirical Support for the Critical Assumptions of Empowerment Theory." *American Journal of Community Psychology* 26 (4): 507–37.

Fox, Paul. 2000. "Passion: The Motive Power in Leadership." *Queen's Quarterly* 107 (1): 8–21.

Franck, Karen A. 1998. "Changing Values in U.S. Public Housing Policy and Design." In *New Directions in Urban Public Housing,* edited by David P. Varady, Wolfgang F. E. Preiser, and Francis P. Russell, 85–104. New Brunswick, N.J.: Center for Urban Policy Research.

Frazier, E. Franklin. 1957. *Black Bourgeoisie.* Glencoe, Ill.: Free Press.

Friedelbaum, Stanley H. 2003. "State Equal Protection: Its Diverse Guises and Effects." *Albany Law Review* 66 (3): 599–633.

Fuller-Thomson, Esme, and Meredith Minkler. 2003. "Housing Issues and Realities Facing Grandparent Caregivers Who Are Renters." *Gerontologist* 43 (1): 92–99.

Fussell, Elizabeth, and Anne H. Gauthier. 2003. "Introduction: Dimensions of Children's Inequality." *Journal of Comparative Family Studies* 34 (3): 311–21.

Galloway, Russell W. 1991. *Justice for All? The Rich and Poor in Supreme Court History 1790–1990.* Raleigh, N.C.: Carolina Academic Press.

Galster, George G. 1990. "Racial Discrimination in Housing Markets during the 1980s: A Review of the Audit Evidence." *Journal of Planning Education and Research* 9 (3): 165–75.

Gilens, Martin. 2003. "How the Poor Became Black: The Racialization of American Poverty in the Mass Media." In *Race and the Politics of Welfare Reform,* edited by Sanford F. Schram, Joe Soss, and Richard C. Fording, 101–30. Ann Arbor: University of Michigan Press.

Gilkes, Cheryl Townsend. 1983. "From Slavery to Social Welfare: Racism and the Control of Black Women." In *Class, Race, and Sex: The Dynamics of Control,* edited by Amy Swerdlow and Hanna Lessinger, 288–300. New York: G. K. Hall.

Gittell, Ross, and Avis Vidal. 1998. *Community Organizing: Building Social Capital as a Development Strategy*. Thousand Oaks, Calif.: Sage.

Glass, J. Conrad, Jr., and Terry L. Huneycutt. 2002. "Grandparents Raising Grandchildren: The Courts, Custody, and Educational Implications." *Educational Gerontology* 28:237–51.

Goering, John, and Modibo Coulibably. 1991. "Public Housing Segregation in the United States." In *Urban Housing Segregation of Minorities in Western Europe and the United States*, edited by Elizabeth D. Huttman, Wim Blauw, and Juliet Saltman, 333–67. Durham, N.C.: Duke University Press.

Goffman, Erving. 1963. *Stigma: Notes on the Management of Spoiled Identity*. New York: Simon & Schuster.

Goldin, Claudia. 1990. *Understanding the Gender Gap*. Oxford: Oxford University Press.

Goode, William J. 1960. "A Theory of Role Strain." *American Sociological Review* 35:483–96.

Gooden, Susan T. 1998. "All Things Not Being Equal: Differences in Caseworker Support toward Black and White Welfare Clients." *Harvard Journal of African-American Public Policy* 4:23–33.

Gooden, Susan T., and Margo Bailey. 2001. "Welfare and Work: Job-Retention Outcomes of Federal Welfare-to-Work Employees." *Public Administration Review* 6 (1): 83.

Gotanda, Neil. 1995. "A Critique of 'Our Constitution is Color-Blind.'" In *Critical Race Theory: Key Writings That Formed the Movement*, edited by Kimberlé Crenshaw, Neil Gotanda, Gary Peller, and Kendall Thomas, 257–75. New York: New Press.

———. 1998. "Tales of Two Judges: Joyce Karlin in People v. Soon Ja Du; Lance Ito in People v. O. J. Simpson." In *The House That Race Built*, edited by Wahneema Lubiano, 66–86. New York: Random House.

Gotham, Kevin Fox. 2000a. "Racialization and the State: The Housing Act of 1934 and the Creation of Federal Housing Administration." *Sociological Perspectives* 43 (2): 291–317.

———. 2000b. "Urban Space, Restrictive Covenants and the Origins of Racial Residential Segregation in a US City, 1900–50." *International Journal of Urban and Regional Research* 24 (3): 616–33.

Gotham, Kevin Fox, and Krista Brumley. 2002. "Using Space: Agency and Identity in a Public-Housing Development." *City and Community* 1 (3): 267–91.

Gould, Mark. 1999. "Race and Theory: Culture, Poverty, and Adaptation to Discrimination in Wilson and Ogbu." *Sociological Theory* 17 (2): 171–200.

Gran, Peter. 1996. *Beyond Eurocentrism: A New View of Modern World History*. Syracuse, N.Y.: Syracuse University Press.

Green, Gary Paul, and Anna Haines. 2002. *Asset Building and Community Development*. Thousand Oaks, Calif.: Sage.

Green, Robert P., Jr., ed. 2000. *Equal Protection: The African-American Constitutional Experience*. New York: Greenwood.

Grice, George L., and John F. Skinner. 1998. *Mastering Public Speaking*. 3rd ed. Boston: Allyn & Bacon.

Grusky, David B., ed. 1994. *Social Stratification in Sociological Perspective*. New York: Westview.

Guba, Egon G., ed. 1990. *The Paradigm Dialog*. New York: Sage.

Gurvitch, Georges. 2000. *Sociology of Law*. New York: Transaction.

Gusfield, Joseph R. 1975. *Community: A Critical Response*. Oxford, UK: Blackwell.

Haistead, Ted, and Michael Lind. 2002. "Unity and Community in the Twenty-First Century." *National Civic Review* 9:95–110.

Harris, Cheryl I. 2002. "Critical Race Studies: An Introduction." *UCLA Law Review* 49 (1215).

———. 2003. "Mining in Hard Ground." Review of *The Miner's Canary*, by Lani Guinier and Gerald Torres. *Harvard Law Review* 116 (8): 2487–539.

Harris, David R. 2001. "Why Are Whites and Blacks Averse to Black Neighbors?" *Social Science Research* 30:100–16.

Harrison, Roderick J., and Daniel H. Weinberg. 1992. "Racial and Ethnic Residential Segregation: 1990." In *Separate and Unequal: The Neighborhood Gap for Blacks and Hispanics in Metropolitan America*, report by the Lewis Mumford Center, October 15, 2002. Retrieved

March 3, 2003.http://mumford1.dyndns.org/cen2000/SepUneq/SUReport/SURepPage1. htm.

Hartman, Chester W. 1975. *Housing and social policy*. Englewood Cliffs, NJ: Prentice Hall.

Harvey, David. 1990. *The Condition of Postmodernity: An Enquiry into the Origins of Cultural Change*. Malden, Mass.: Blackwell.

Hashima, Patricia Y., and Paul R. Amato. 1994. "Poverty, Social Support, and Parental Behavior." *Child Development* 65 (2): 394–404.

Hawe, Penelope, and Alan Shiel. 2000. "Social Capital and Health Promotion: A Review." *Social Science and Medicine* 51:871–85.

Hays, R. Allen. 1995. *The Federal Government and Urban Housing: Ideology and Change in Public Policy*. Albany, N.Y.: State University of New York.

Hellegers, Adam P. 1999. "Reforming HUD's 'One-Strike' Public Housing Evictions through Tenant Participation." *Journal of Criminal Law and Criminology* 90 (1): 323.

Hensen, Julia L., and Franklin J. James. 1987. "Housing Discrimination in Small Cities and Nonmetropolitan Areas." In *Divided Neighborhoods: Changing Patterns of Racial Segregation*, edited by Gary A. Tobin, 181–208. Newbury Park, Calif.: Sage.

Hines, Revathi I. 2001. "African-Americans' Struggle for Environmental Justice and the Case of the Shintech Plant: Lessons Learned from a War Waged." *Journal of Black Studies* 31 (6): 777–89.

Hochschild. Jennifer L. 1995. *Facing Up to the American Dream: Race, Class, and the Soul of the Nation*. Princeton, N.J.: Princeton University Press.

Housing Act of 1937. Pub. L. No. 50. 50 Stat. 888.

Housing Act of 1949. Pub. L. No. 38. 63 Stat. 413.

Housing Act of 1961. Pub. L. No. 87-70. 75 Stat. 149.

Housing Act of 1968. Pub. L. No. 90-448. 82 Stat. 476.

Huang, Chien-Chung. 2002. "The Impact of Child Support Enforcement on Nonmarital and Marital Births: Does It Differ by Racial and Age Groups?" *Social Service Review* 76 (2): 275–303.

HUD (U.S. Department of Housing and Urban Development). 1992. *Evaluating the Effectiveness of Tenant Management*. http://www.huduser.org/Publications/pdf/HUD-006093.pdf.

———. 2003a. *Fiscal Year 2004 HUD Budget Executive Summary*. Retrieved March 15, 2003.http://www.hud.gov/about/budget/fy04/execsummary.cfm.

———. 2003b. *Public Housing Occupancy Guidebook*. Washington, D.C.: Office of Public and Indian Housing.

Hughes, Michael, and Bradley R. Hertel. 1990. "The Significance of Color Remains: A Study of Life Chances, Mate Selection, and Ethnic Consciousness among Black Americans." *Social Forces* 68 (4): 1105–17.

Hutchinson, Darren Lenard. 2002. "Critical Race Studies: Progressive Race Blindness? Individual Identity, Group Politics, and Reform." *UCLA Law Review* 49 (5): 1455.

Ihlanfeldt, Keith. 2002. "Spatial Mismatch in the Labor Market and Racial Differences in Neighborhood Crime." *Economics Letters* 76 (1): 73–76.

Ihlanfeldt, Keith and David Sjoquist. 1998. "The Spatial Mismatch Hypothesis: A Review of Recent Studies and Their Implications for Welfare Reform." *Housing Policy Debate* 9 (4): 849–92.

Isaacs, Mareasa R., and Marva P. Benjamin. 1991. *Programs Which Utilize Culturally Competent Principles: Volume II*. Washington, D.C.: CASSP Technical Assistance Center, Georgetown University Child Development Center.

Jacobson, Thomas L. 1998. "Discourse Ethics and the Right to Communicate." *Gazette* 60 (5): 395.

Jaffee D. 2001. *Organization Theory: Tension and Change*. Boston: McGraw-Hill International.

Janowitz, Morris. 1975. "Sociological Theory and Social Control." *American Journal of Sociology* 81 (1): 82–108.

Jawahar, I.M., and G. L. McLaughlin. 2001. "Toward A Descriptive Stakeholder Theory: An Organizational Life Cycle Approach." *Academy of Management Review* 26: 397–414.

Jay, Michelle. 2003. "Critical Race Theory, Multicultural Education, and the Hidden Curriculum of Hegemony." *Multicultural Perspectives* 5 (4): 3–10.

Johnson-Bailey, Juanita.1999. "The Ties That Bind and the Shackles That Separate: Race, Gender, Class, and Color in a Research Process." *Qualitative Studies in Education* 12 (6): 659–70.

Jones-Correa, Michael. 2000. "The Origins and Diffusion of Racial Restrictive Covenants." *Political Science Quarterly* 115 (4): 541–68.

Kaase, Max. 1999. "Interpersonal Trust, Political Trust, and Non-Institutionalized Political Participation in Western Europe." *Western Europe Politics* 22:1–21.

Kaestner, Robert and Wendy Fleischer. 1992. "Income Inequality as an Indicator of Discrimination in Housing Markets." *Review of Black Political Economy* 21 (2): 55–81.

Keating-Lefler, Rebecca, Diane Hudson, Christie Campbell-Grossman, Missy Fleck, and Joan Westfall. 2003. "Needs, Concerns, and Social Support of Single, Low-Income Mothers." *Issues in Mental Health Nursing* 25 (4): 381–412.

Keiser, Lael, Peter R. Mueser, and Seung-Whan Choi. 2004. "Race, Bureaucratic Discretions, and the Implementation of Welfare Reform." *American Journal of Political Science* 48 (1): 314–28.

Kennedy, Randall. 2002. *Nigger: The Strange Career of a Troublesome Word.* New York: Random House.

Kerbo, Harold R. 1996. *Social Stratification and Inequality: Class Conflict in Historical and Comparative Perspective.* 3rd ed. New York: McGraw-Hill.

Kershaw, Terry. 1992. "Toward a Black Studies Paradigm: An Assessment and Some Direction." *Journal of Black Studies* 22 (4): 477–94.

———. 2003. "The Black Studies Paradigm: The Making of Scholar Activist." In *Afrocentricity and the Academy: Essays on Theory and Practice,* edited by James L. Conyers Jr, 27–37. New York: McFarland.

Koebel, C. Theodore, and Marilyn S. Cavell. 1995. *Tenant Organizations in Public Housing Projects: A Report on Senate Resolution No. 347.* Virginia Center for Housing Research. October.

Krivo, Lauren J., and Ruth D. Peterson. 1996. "Extremely Disadvantaged Neighborhoods and Urban Crime." *Social Forces* 75 (2): 619–49.

Krivo, Lauren J., Ruth D. Peterson, Helen Rizzo, and John R. Reynolds. 1998. "Race, Segregation, and the Concentration of Disadvantage: 1980–1990." 45 (1): 61–81.

Kubin, Charis E., and Ronald Weitzer. 2003. "New Directions in Social Disorganization Theory." *Journal of Research in Crime and Delinquency* 40 (4): 374–402.

Kuhn, Thomas. 1970. *The Structure of Scientific Revolutions.* Chicago: University of Chicago Press.

Kuo, Frances E. 2001. "Coping with Poverty: Impacts of Environment and Attention in the Inner City." *Environment and Behavior* 33 (1): 5–35.

Ladner, Joyce A. 1998. *The Death of White Sociology.* New York: Random House.

Ladson-Billings, Gloria. 1998. "Just What Is Critical Race Theory and What's It Doing in a Nice Field Like Education?" *Qualitative Studies in Education* 11 (1): 7–24.

Lane, Vincent. 1995. "Best Management Practices in U.S. Public Housing." *Housing Policy Debate* 6 (4): 867–904.

Lang, Robert E., and Steven Hornburg. 1998. "What Is Social Capital and Why Is It Important to Public Policy." *Housing Policy Debate* 9:1–17.

LaVeist, Thomas A. 1989. "Linking Residential Segregation and the Infant Mortality Race Disparity." *Sociology and Social Research* 73 (2): 90–94.

LaVeist, Thomas A., and John M. Wallace. 2000. "Health Risk and Inequitable Distribution of Liquor Stores in African-American Neighborhoods." *Social Science and Medicine* 51 (4): 613–17.

Leahy, James E. 1992. *Liberty, Justice, and Equality: How These Constitutional Guarantees Have Been Shaped by United States Supreme Court Decisions since 1789.* Jefferson, N.C.: McFarland.

Lee, Evelyn. 1997. *Working with Asian Americans: A Guide for Clinicians.* New York: Guilford.

Lemann, Nicholas. 1991. *The Promised Land: The Great Black Migration and How It Changed America*. New York: Knopf.

Lemert, Charles, ed. 1993. *Social Theory: The Multicultural and Classic Readings*. New York: Westview.

Lessig, Lawrence. 1995. "The Regulation of Social Meaning." *University of Chicago Law Review* 62 (943).

Leventhal, Tama, and Jeanne Brooks-Gunn. 2003. "Moving to Opportunity: An Experimental Study of Neighborhood Effects on Mental Health." *American Journal of Public Health* 93 (9): 1576–84.

Lewis, Amanda E. 2003. "Everyday Race-Making: Navigating Racial Boundaries in Schools." *American Behavioral Scientist* 47 (3): 283–305.

Lewis, Oscar. 1969. "The Culture of Poverty." In *On Understanding Poverty: Perspectives from the Social Sciences*, edited by Daniel P. Moynihan, 187–200. New York: Basic.

———. 1998. "The Culture of Poverty." *Society* 35 (2): 7–11.

Lewis Mumford Center. 2001. *Ethnic Diversity Grows, Neighborhood Integration Is at a Standstill.* Report by the Lewis Mumford Center, April 3. Retrieved March 3, 2003.http://mumford1.dyndns.org/Cens200/WholePop/Wpreport/page1.html.

Lieberman, Robert C. 1995. "Race and the Organization of Welfare Policy." In *Classifying by Race*, edited by Paul E. Peterson, 156–87. Princeton, N.J.: Princeton University Press.

Lin, Nan. 2001. *Social Capital: A Theory of Social Structure and Action*. New York: Cambridge University Press.

Lincoln, Yvonna S., and Egon G. Guba. 1985. *Naturalistic Inquiry*. Thousand Oaks, Calif.: Sage.

Lipsitz, George L. 1998. *The Possessive Investment in Whiteness: How White People Profit from Identity Politics*. Philadelphia: Temple University Press.

Lively, Donald E. 1992. *The Constitution and Race*. New York: Praeger.

Lloyd, B. 1996. "Power, Responsibility, Leadership and Learning: The Need For an Integrated Approach." *Leadership and Organization Development Journal* 17 (4): 52–57.

Lober, Judith. 1999. "Embattled Terrain: Gender and Sexuality." In Myra Marx Ferree, Judith Lorber, and Beth B. Hess. *Revisioning Gender*, 416–48. Thousand Oaks, Calif.: Sage.

Lochner, Kimberly A., Ichiro Kawachi, Robert T. Brennan, and Stephen L. Buka. 2003. "Social Capital and Neighborhood Mortality Rates in Chicago." *Social Science and Medicine* 56:1797–99.

Lominger, Michael M. 2004. "The Blueprint for Enduring Success at the Top." Lominger.com. Retrieved November 1, 2004. www.lominger.com.

Lubiano, Wahneema, ed. 1998. *The House That Race Built*. New York: Random House.

Lundy, Garvey F. 2003. "The Myths of Oppositional Culture." *Journal of Black Studies* 33 (4): 450–67.

Lynn, Marvin. 1999. "Toward a Critical Race Pedagogy: A Research Note." *Urban Education* 33 (5): 606–26.

Macleod, Catriona, and Kevin Durrheim. 2002. "Racializing Teenage Pregnancy: 'Culture' and 'Tradition' in the South African Scientific Literature." *Ethnic and Racial Studies* 25 (5): 778–801.

Macionis, John J, and Vincent N. Parrillo. 2004. *Cities and Urban Life*. 3rd edition. Upper Saddle River, NJ: Prentice Hall.

Maines, David. 2000. "The Social Construction of Meaning." *Contemporary Sociology* 29 (4): 577–84.

Major, Debra A. 2003. "Utilizing Role Theory to Help Employed Parents Cope with Children's Chronic Illness." *Health Education Research: Theory and Practice* 18 (1): 45–57.

Manpower Demonstration Research Corporation. 1981. *Tenant Management: Findings from a Three-Year Experiment in Public Housing*. Cambridge, Mass.: Ballinger.

Marcuse, Peter. 1998. "Mainstreaming Public Housing: A Proposal for a Comprehensive Approach to Housing Policy." In *New Directions in Urban Public Housing*, edited by David P. Varady, Wolfgang F. E. Preiser, and Francis P. Russell, 47–61. New Brunswick, N.J.: Center for Urban Policy Research.

Martinez, Sylvia. 2000. "The Housing Act of 1949: Its Place in the Realization of the American Dream of Homeownership." *Housing Policy Debate* 11:467–86.

Martinot, Steve. 2003. *The Rule of Racialization: Class, Identity, Governance.* Philadelphia: Temple University Press.

Massey, Douglas S. 2001. "Residential Segregation and Neighborhood Conditions in US Metropolitan Areas." In *America Becoming: Racial Trends and Their Consequences*, edited by Neil J. Smelser, William Julius Wilson, and Faith Mitchell, 391–434. Washington, D.C.: National Academy Press.

Massey, Douglas S., and Nancy A. Denton. 1988a. "Dimensions of Residential Segregation." *Social Forces* 67 (2): 281–361.

———. 1988b. "Suburbanization and Segregation in U.S. Metropolitan Areas." *American Journal of Sociology* 94 (3): 592–627.

———. 1993. *American Apartheid: Segregation and the Making of the Underclass.* Cambridge, Mass.: Harvard University Press.

Massey, Douglas S., and Shawn Kanaiaupuni. 1993. "Public Housing and the Concentration of Poverty." *Social Science Quarterly* 74 (1): 109–13.

Matsuda, Mari. 1991. "Voices of America: Accent, Antidiscrimination Law, and a Jurisprudence for the Last Reconstruction." *Yale Law Journal* 100:1329–1407.

Matsuda, Mari J., Charles R. Lawrence III, Richard Delgado, and Kimberlé Williams Crenshaw. 1993. *Words That Wound: Critical Race Theory, Assaultive Speech, and the First Amendment.* New York: Westview.

McAdoo, Harriette P. 1997. *Black Families.* 3rd ed. Thousand Oaks, Calif.: Sage.

McAllister, Lydia E., and Joyceen S. Boyle. 1998. "Without Money, Means, or Men: African-American Women Receiving Prenatal Care in a Housing Project." *Family and Community Health* 21(3).

McNamara, Carter. 2004. "Suggested Competencies for Effective Leadership Skills in Organizations." Authenticity Consulting LLC. Retrieved November 5, 2004.http://www. authenticityconsulting.com/.

McNulty, Thomas L., and Steven R. Holloway. 2000. "Race, Crime, and Public Housing in Atlanta: Testing a Conditional Effect Hypothesis." *Social Forces* 79 (2): 707–32.

Meier, Robert F. 1982. "Perspectives on the Concept of Social Control." *Annual Review of Sociology* 8:35–55.

Merriam, Sharan B. 2001. *Qualitative Research and Case Study Applications in Education.* San Francisco: Jossey-Bass.

Meyer, Stephen Grant. 2000. *As Long as They Don't Move Next Door.* Lanham, Md.: Rowman & Littlefield.

Mills, C. Wright. 1956. *The Power Elite.* Oxford: Oxford University Press.

Minow, Martha. 1990. *Making All the Difference: Inclusion, Exclusion, and American Law.* Ithaca, N.Y.: Cornell University Press.

Mitchell, Duneier. 1992. *Slim's Table: Race, Respectability, and Masculinity.* Chicago: University of Chicago Press.

Morse, Janice M. 1998. "Designing Funded Qualitative Research." In *Strategies for Qualitative Inquiry*, edited by Norman K. Denzin and Yvonna S. Lincoln, 56–86. London: Sage.

Mussig, Dennis J. 2003. "A Research and Skills Training for Values-Driven Leadership." *Journal of European Industrial Training* 27 (2): 73–80.

National Commission on Severely Distressed Public Housing. 1992. *The Final Report of the National Commission on Severely Distressed Public Housing: A Report to the Congress and the Secretary of Housing and Urban Development.* Washington, D.C.: U.S. Government Publishing Office.

National Joint Committee for the Communicative Needs of Persons with Severe Disabilities. 1992. *Guidelines for Meeting the Communication Needs of Persons with Severe Disabilities. American Speech Language and Hearing Association (ASHA)* 34 (March, Supp. 7): 1–8.

Neubeck, Kenneth J., and Noel A. Cazenave. 2001. *Welfare Racism: Playing the Race Card against America's Poor.* New York: Routledge.

Neuman, W. Lawrence. 1997. *Social Research Methods: Qualitative and Quantitative Approaches.* Needham Heights, Mass.: Allyn & Bacon.

Neville, Helen A., and Jennifer Hamer. 2001. "We Make Freedom: An Exploration of Revolutionary Black Feminism." *Journal of Black Studies* 31:437–61.

Newman, Sandra J., ed. 1999. *The Home Front: Implications of Welfare Reform for Housing Policy.* Washington, D.C.: Urban Institute.

Oliver, Melvin L. and Thomas M. Shapiro. 1995. *Black Wealth/White Wealth: A New Perspective on Racial Inequality.* New York: Routledge.

Omi, Michael, and Howard Winant. 1994. *Racial Formation in the United States: From 1960s to the 1990s.* New York: Routledge.

Parker, Laurence and Marvin Lynn. 2002. "What's Race Got to Do with It? Critical Race Theory's Conflicts with and Connections to Qualitative Research Methodology and Epistemology." *Qualitative Inquiry* 8 (1): 7–22.

Patton, Michael Quinn. 1990. *Qualitative Evaluation and Research Methods.* Newbury Park, Calif.: Sage.

———. 2002. *Qualitative Research and Evaluative Methods.* 3rd ed. Newbury Park, Calif.: Sage.

Pattillo-McCoy, Mary. 1999. *Black Picket Fences: Privilege and Peril among the Black Middle Class.* Chicago: University of Chicago Press.

Peller, Gary. 1995. "Race-Consciousness." In *Critical Race Theory: The Key Writings That Formed The Movement,* edited by Kimberlé Crenshaw, Neil Gotanda, Gary Peller, and Kendall Thomas, 127–58. New York: New Press.

Peterman, William. 1996. "The Meaning of Resident Empowerment: Why Just about Everybody Thinks It's a Good Idea and What It Has to Do with Resident Management." *Housing Policy Debate* 7 (3): 473–90.

———. 2000. *Neighborhood Planning and Community-Based Development: The Potential and Limits of Grassroots Action.* Thousand Oaks, Calif.: Sage.

Piña, Darlene L., and Vern L. Bengtson. 1993. "The Division of Household Labor and Wives' Happiness: Ideology, Employment and Perceptions of Support." *Journal of Marriage and the Family* 55 (4): 901–12.

Pinderhughes, Raquel. 1996. "The Impact of Race on Environmental Quality: An Empirical and Theoretical Discussion." *Sociological Perspectives* 39 (2): 231–48.

Pirog, Maureen A., Marilyn E. Klotz, and Katharine V. Byers. 1998. "Interstate Comparisons of Child Support Orders Using State Guidelines." *Family Relations* 47 (3): 289–295.

Piven, Frances Fox, and Richard A. Cloward. 1993. *Regulating the Poor: The Functions of Public Welfare.* New York: Vintage.

———. 1997. *The Breaking of the American Social Compact.* New York: New Press.

Portes, Alejandro. 1998. "Social Capital: Its Origins and Applications in Modern Sociology." *Annual Review of Sociology* 24:1–24.

Potapchuk, William R., Jarle P. Crocker, and William H. Schechter. 1997. "Building Community with Social Capital: Chits and Chums or Chats with Change." *National Civic Review* 86:129–39.

Proctor, Bernadette D., and Joseph Dalaker. 2003. *Poverty in the United States: 2002.* Washington, D.C.: U.S. Government Publishing Office, 1–33.

Purdy, Sean. 2003. "'It Was Tough on Everybody': Low-Income Families and Housing Hardship in Post–World War II Toronto." *Journal of Social History* 37 (2): 457–85.

Putnam, Robert D. 1993. "The Prosperous Community: Social Capital and Public Life." *American Prospect* 13:35–42.

———. 1995. "Bowling Alone: America's Declining Social Capital." *Journal of Democracy* 6:65–78.

———. 1998. Foreword. *Housing Policy Debate* 9:v–viii.

Putnam, Robert D., Robert Leonardi, and Raffaellay Nanetti. 1993. *Making Democracy Work: Civic Traditions in Modern Italy.* Princeton, N.J.: Princeton University Press.

Quillian, Lincoln. 2002. "Why Is Black-White Residential Segregation So Persistent? Evidence on Three Theories from Migration Data." *Social Science Research* 31:197–229.

Radford, Gail. 1998. *Modern Housing for America.* Chicago: University of Chicago Press.

Ralph, James. R. 1993. *Northern Protest: Martin Luther King Jr., Chicago, and the Civil Rights Movement.* Cambridge, Mass.: Harvard University Press.

Rank, Mark R. 2001. "The Effects of Poverty on America's Families: Assessing Our Research Knowledge." *Journal of Family Issues* 22 (7): 882–903.

Rankin, Bruce H., and James M. Quane. 2000. "Neighborhood Poverty and the Social Isolation of Inner City African-American Families." *Social Forces* 79 (1): 139–64.

Raphael, Dennis, Rebecca Renwick, Ivan Brown, Brenda Steinmetz, Hersh Sehdev, and Sherry Phillips. 2001. "Making the Links between Community Structure and Individual Well-Being: Community Quality of Life in Riverdale, Toronto, Canada." *Health and Place* 7:179–96.

Reichl, Alexander J. 1999. "Learning from St. Thomas: Community, Capital, and Redevelopment of Public Housing in New Orleans." *Journal of Urban Affairs* 21 (2): 169–87.

Roberts, Dorothy. 1995. "Punishing Drug Addicts Who Have Babies: Women of Color, Equality, and the Right of Privacy." In *Critical Race Theory: The Key Writings That Formed the Movement*, edited by Kimberlé Crenshaw, Neil Gotanda, Gary Peller, and Kendall Thomas, 384–425. New York: New Press.

———. 2002. *Shattered Bonds: The Color of Child Welfare*. New York: Basic Civitas.

Roemer, John E. 2000. "Equality of Opportunity." In *Meritocracy and Economic Inequality*, edited by Kenneth Arrow, Samuel Bowles, and Steven Durlauf, 17–33. Princeton, N.J.: Princeton University Press.

Rollins, Joan H., Renee N. Saris, and Ingrid Johnston-Robledo. 2001. "Low-Income Women Speak Out about Housing: A High-Stakes Game of Musical Chairs." *Journal of Social Issues* 57 (2): 277.

Romer, Daniel, Kathleen H. Jamieson, and Nicole J. DeCoteau. 1998. "The Treatment of People of Color in Local Television News—Ethnic Blame Discourse or Realist Group Conflict." *Communication Research* 25:286–305.

Rosenbaum, Emily, and Laura E. Harris. 2001. "Low-Income Families in Their New Neighborhoods: The Short-Term Effects of Moving from Chicago's Public Housing." *Journal of Family Issues* 22 (2): 183–210.

Rosenfeld, Richard, Bruce A. Jacobs, and Richard Wright. 2003. "Snitching and the Code of the Street." *British Journal of Criminology* 43 (2): 291–309.

Ross, Stephen, and John Yinger. 2002. *The Color of Credit: Mortgage Discrimination, Research Methodology, and Fair-Lending Enforcement*. Cambridge, Mass.: MIT Press.

Rozario, Philip A., Nancy Morrow-Howell, and James E. Hinterlong. 2004. "Role Enhancement or Role Strain: Assessing the Impact of Multiple Productive Roles on Older Caregiver Well-Being." *Research on Aging* 26 (4): 413–29.

Ruckers v. Davis (US Dist. Lexis 9345[1998]).

Rush, Ladonna L. 1998. "Affective Reactions to Multiple Social Stigmas." *Journal of Social Psychology* 138 (4): 421–31.

Rushefsky, Mark E. 2002. *Public Policy in the United States: At the Dawn of the Twenty- First Century*. New York: Sharpe.

Salins, Peter D., ed. 1987. *Housing America's Poor*. Chapel Hill: University of North Carolina Press.

Samborn, Hope Viner. 1999. "Child Support for Grandma: When Grandparents Raise the Kids, Parents Increasingly Are Being Made to Pay the Tab." *American Bar Association* 85:28.

Sampson, Robert J. 2001. "What Community Supplies." In *Community Organizing and Development*, edited by Herbert J. Rubin and Irene S. Rubin, 241–92. Boston: Allyn & Bacon.

Schansberg, D. Eric. 1996. *Poor Policy: How Government Harms the Poor*. Boulder, Colo.: Westview.

Scheppele, Kim Lane. 1994. "Legal Theory and Social Theory." *Annual Review Sociology* 20:383–406.

Schnee, David M. 1998. "An Evaluation of Robert Pits Plaza: A Post-Occupancy Evaluation of New Public Housing in San Francisco." In *New Directions in Urban Public Housing*, edited by David P. Varady, Wolfgang F. E. Preiser, and Francis P. Russell, 104–21. New Brunswick, N.J.: Center for Urban Policy Research.

Schorr, Alvin L. 2001. *Welfare Reform: Failure and Remedies*. Westport, Conn.: Praeger.

Schur, Richard. 2002. "Critical Race Theory and the Limits of Auto/Bibliography: Reading Patricia William's *The Alchemy of Race and Rights* through/against Postcolonial Theory." *Biography* 25 (3): 455–78.

Schwalbe, Michael, Sandra Godwin, Daphne Holden, Douglas Schrock, and Shealy Thompson. 2000. "Generic Processes in the Reproduction of Inequality: An Interactionist Analysis." *Social Forces* 79 (2): 419–53.

Schwartz, Alex F. 2015. *Housing Policy in the United States*. New York: Routledge.

Seiler, Naomi. 2003. "Identifying Racial Privilege: Lessons from Critical Race Theory and the Law." *American Journal of Bioethics* 3 (2): 24–25.

Seitles, Marc. 1996. "The Perpetuation of Residential Racial Segregation in America: Historical Discrimination, Modern Forms of Exclusion, and Inclusionary Remedies." *Journal of Land Use and Environmental Law*.

Seron, Carroll, and Frank Munger. 1994. "Law and Inequality: Race, Gender . . . and, of Course, Class." *Annual Review of Sociology* 22:187–212.

Shihadeh, Edward S., and Nicole Flynn. 1996. "Segregation and Crime: The Effect of Black Social Isolation on the Rates of Black Urban Violence." *Social Forces* 74 (4): 1325–52.

Sieber, Sam D. 1974. "Toward a Theory of Role Accumulation." *American Sociological Review* 39:567–78.

Slessarev, Helene. 1997. *The Betrayal of the Urban Poor*. Philadelphia: Temple University Press.

Smelser, Neil J., William Julius Wilson, and Faith Mitchell, eds. 2001. *America Becoming: Racial Trends and Their Consequences*. Vol. 1. Washington D.C.: National Academy Press.

Smith, Janet L. 1999. "Cleaning Up Public Housing by Sweeping Out the Poor." *Habitat International* 23 (1): 49–62.

Smith, Neal, Lori Baugh Littlejohns, and Donna Thompson. 2001. "Shaking Out the Cobwebs: Insight into Community Capacity and Its Relations to Health Outcomes." *Community Development Journal* 36:30–42.

Souza Briggs, Xavier de. 1997. "Social Capital and the Cities: Advice to Change Agents." *National Civic Review* 86 (2): 111–18.

Stake, Robert E. 2000. "Case Studies." In *Handbook of Qualitative Research*, edited by Norman K. Denzin and Yvonna S. Lincoln, 435–54. Thousand Oaks, Calif.: Sage.

Stall, Susan, and Randy Stoecker. 1998. "Community Organizing or Organizing Community? Gender and the Crafts of Empowerment." *Gender and Society* 12 (6): 729–56.

Stegman, Michael A. 1995. "Recent US Urban Change and Policy Initiatives." *Urban Studies* 32 (10): 1601–8.

Steinberg, Stephen. 2001. *The Ethnic Myth: Race, Ethnicity, and Class in America*. 3rd ed. Boston: Beacon.

Stier, Haya, and Marta Tienda. 2001. *The Color of Opportunity: Pathways to Family, Welfare, and Work*. Chicago: University of Chicago Press.

Stohs, Joanne Hoven. 2000. "Multicultural Women's Experience of Household Labor, Conflicts, and Equity." *Sex Roles: A Journal of Research* 42 (5/6): 339–62.

Stone, Blair Cameron. 1986. "Community, Home, and the Residential Tenant." *University of Pennsylvania Law Review* 134 (627).

Stone, Michael E. 1993. *Shelter Poverty: New Ideas on Housing Affordability*. Philadelphia: Temple University Press.

Sutermeister, Oscar. 1969. "Inadequacies and Inconsistencies in the Definition of Substandard Housing." In *Housing Coed Standards: Three Critical Studies*, National Commission on Urban Problems, Research Report no. 19, 82–102.

Suttles, Gerald D. 1972. *The Social Construction of Communities*. Chicago: University of Chicago Press.

Squires, Gregory D., Samantha Friedman, and Catherine E. Saidat. 2002. "Experiencing Residential Segregation: A Contemporary Study of Washington, D.C." *Urban Affairs Review* 38 (2): 155–83.

Takaki, Ronald. 1993. *A Different Mirror: A History of Multicultural America*. Boston: Little, Brown.

Tatum, Beverly. 1997. *Why Are All the Black Kids Sitting Together in the Cafeteria? And Other Conversations about Race.* New York: Basic.

Temkin, Kenneth, and William M. Rohe. 1998. "Social Capital and Neighborhood Stability: An Empirical Investigation." *Housing Policy Debate* 9:61–88.

Thomas, Anita J., Karen M. Witherspoon, and Suzette L. Speight. 2004. "Toward the Development of the Stereotypic Roles for Black Women Scale." *Journal of Black Psychology* 30 (3): 426–42.

Thomas, Melvin, and Michael Hughes. 1986. "The Continuing Significance of Race: A Study of Race, Class, and Quality of Life in America, 1972–1982." *American Sociological Review* 51: 830–41.

Tobin, Gary A., ed. 1987. *Divided Neighborhoods: Changing Patterns of Racial Segregation.* Newbury Park, Calif.: Sage.

United States Bureau of the Census. 2002a. *Money Income in the United States: 2001.* Report by Carmen DeNavas-Walt and Robert D. Cleveland. Retrieved March 15, 2003.http://www.census.gov/prod/2002pubs/p60-218.pdf.

United States Bureau of the Census. 2002b. *Statistical Abstract of the United States: 2002.* 122nd ed. Washington, D.C.

United States Federal Housing Administration. 1938. *Underwriting Manual.* Washington, D.C.: U.S. Government Publishing Office.

Valdes, Francisco, Merome McCristal Culp, and Angela P. Harris, eds. 2002. *Crossroads, Directions, and a New Critical Race Theory.* Philadelphia: Temple University Press.

Vale, Lawrence J. 1998. "Public Housing and the American Dream: Residents' Views on Buying Into the Projects." *Housing Policy Debate* 9 (2): 267–98.

———. 2000. *From the Puritans to the Projects: Public Housing and Public Neighbors.* Cambridge, Mass.: Harvard University Press.

Van Deburg, William L., ed. 1997. *Modern Black Nationalism: From Marcus Garvey to Louis Farrakhan.* New York: New York University Press.

Van Maanen, John, James M. Dabbs, and Robert R. Faulkner. 1982. *Varieties of Qualitative Research.* Beverly Hills, Calif.: Sage.

Vanneman, Reeve, and Lynn W. Cannon. 1987. *The American Perception of Class.* Philadelphia: Temple University Press.

Van Ryzin, Gregg, Michelle Ronda, and Douglas Muzzio. 2001. "Factors Related to Self-Sufficiency in a Distressed Public Housing Community." *Journal of Urban Affairs* 23 (1): 57–69.

Varady, David P., Wolfgang F. E. Preiser, and Francis P. Russell, eds. 1998. *New Directions in Urban Public Housing.* New Brunswick, N.J.: Center for Urban Policy Research.

Venkatesh, Sudhir Alladi. 1997. "An Invisible Community: Inside Chicago's Public Housing." *American Prospect* 34:34–41.

———. 2000. *American Project: The Rise and Fall of a Modern Metropolis.* Cambridge, Mass.: Harvard University Press.

Von Hoffman, Alexander. 1997. "Good News: From Boston to San Francisco the Community Based Housing Movement Is Transforming Bad Neighborhoods." *Atlantic Monthly* 279:31–35.

———. 1998. "High Ambitions: The Past and Future of American Low-Income Housing Policy." In *New Directions in Urban Public Housing,* edited by David P. Varady, Wolfgang F. E. Preiser, and Francis P. Russell, 3–23. New Brunswick, N.J.: Center for Urban Policy Research.

———. 2000. "A Study in Contradictions: The Origins and Legacy of the Housing Act of 1949." *Housing Policy Debate* 11 (2): 299–326.

Weber, Lynn. 2001. *Understanding Race, Class, Gender, and Sexuality: A Conceptual Framework.* New York: McGraw-Hill.

Weinberg, Bruce A. 2000. "Black Residential Centralization and the Spatial Mismatch Hypothesis." *Journal of Urban Economics* 48:110–34.

Weinberg, Z., and M. Epstein. 1996. *No Place to Shop.* Washington, D.C.: Public Voice for Food and Healthy Policy.

Welfeld, Irving H. 1992. *HUD Scandals: Howling Headlines and Silent Fiascoes*. New Brunswick, N.J.: Transaction.

Wells, Richard H., and J. Steven Picou. 1981. *American Sociology: Theoretical and Methodological Structure*. Washington D.C.: University Press of America.

Wilkerson, Isabel. 1988. "From Squalor to Showcase: One Tenant Group's Success." *New York Times*, June 11. Retrieved November 21, 2001.http://web.lexis-nexis.com/universe.

Williams, David R., and Chiquita Collins. 2001. "Racial Residential Segregation: A Fundamental Cause of Racial Disparities in Health." *Public Health Reports* 116 (5): 404–17.

Williams, Patricia J. 2001. *The Alchemy of Race and Rights*. Cambridge, Mass.: Harvard University Press.

Wilson, William J. 1980. *The Declining Significance of Race: Blacks and Changing American Institutions*. 2nd ed. Chicago: University of Chicago Press.

———. 1987. *The Truly Disadvantaged: The Inner City, the Underclass, and Public Policy*. Chicago: University of Chicago Press.

———. 1991. "Studying Inner-City Social Dislocations: The Challenge of Public Agenda Research: 1990 Presidential Address." *American Sociological Review* 56 (1): 1–14.

———. 1996. *When Work Disappears: The World of the New Urban Poor*. New York: Vintage.

———. 1998. "Inner-City Dislocations." *Society* 35 (2): 270–78.

Wilson, William J., and Robert Aponte. 1985. "Urban Poverty." *Annual Review of Sociology* 11:231–58.

Winant, Howard. 1998. "Racial Dualism at Century's End." In *The House That Race Built*, edited by Wahneema Lubiano, 87–115. New York: Random House.

Wing, Adrien K., ed. 1997. *Critical Race Feminism: A Reader*. New York: New York University Press.

Wolff, Thomas. 2001. "Community Coalition Building—Contemporary Practice and Research." *American Journal of Community Psychology* 29 (2): 165–73.

Wolk, James L., and Sandra Schmahl. 1999. "Child Support Enforcement: The Ignored Component of Welfare Reform." *Families in Society: The Journal of Contemporary Human Services* 80 (5): 526–40.

Yamamoto, Eric K. 1997. "Critical Race Praxis: Race Theory and Political Lawyering Practice in Post–Civil Rights America." *Michigan Law Review* 95 (4): 821–900.

Yinger, John. 1986. "Measuring Racial Discrimination with Fair Housing Audits: Caught in the Act." *American Economic Review* 76:881–94.

———. 1987. "The Racial Dimension of Urban Housing Markets in the 1980s." In *Divided Neighborhoods: Changing Patterns of Racial Segregation*, edited by Gary A. Tobin, 43–68. Newbury Park, Calif.: Sage.

———. 1998. "Housing Discrimination Is Still Worth Worrying About." *Housing Policy Debate* 9 (4) :893–927.

———. 1999. "Testing for Discrimination in Housing and Related Markets." In *A National Report Card on Discrimination in America: The Role of Testing*, edited by Michael Fix and Margery Austin Turner, 27–46. Washington, D.C.: Urban Institute.

Zenou, Yves, and Nicolas Boccard. 2000. "Racial Discrimination and Redlining in Cities." *Journal of Urban Economics* 48: 260–85.

Zukin, Sharon. 1998. "How 'Bad' Is It? Institutions and Intentions in the Study of the American Ghetto." *International Journal of Urban and Regional Research* 22:511–20.

Index

About the Author

Tiffany G. Chenault (PhD, Virginia Tech) received her doctorate and master's degree in sociology with a concentration in social inequality and race and social policy. Currently, Dr. Chenault is an associate professor at Salem State University and serves as a board member of Alternatives for Community and Empowerment, which works with communities of color and low-income communities in Massachusetts to eradicate environmental racism and classism; create healthy, sustainable communities; and achieve environmental justice. Her research interest includes voting inequalities, along with racial and gender dynamics in the workplace and in communities.

CPSIA information can be obtained at www.ICGtesting.com
Printed in the USA
BVOW02*1637310715

410831BV00003BB/4/P